Helion & Company Limited
Unit 8 Amherst Business Centre
Budbrooke Road
Warwick
CV34 5WE
England
Tel. 01926 499 619
Email: info@helion.co.uk
Website: www.helion.co.uk
Twitter: @helionbooks
https://helionbooks.wordpress.com/

Cover: A battery of 105mm howitzers of the Groupement Mobile B Task Force of the counter-coup forces of Gen Phoumi Nosavan opening fire on a Neutralist blocking position along Route 13 during their drive to reconquer Vientiane in December 1960. (Albert Grandolini Collection)

Designed and typeset by Mach 3 Solutions (www.mach3solutions.co.uk)
Cover design Paul Hewitt, Battlefield Design (www.battlefield-design.co.uk)

ISBN: 978-1-804518-63-2

British Library Cataloguing-in-Publication Data
A catalogue record for this book is available from the British Library

We always welcome receiving book proposals from prospective authors.

CONTENTS

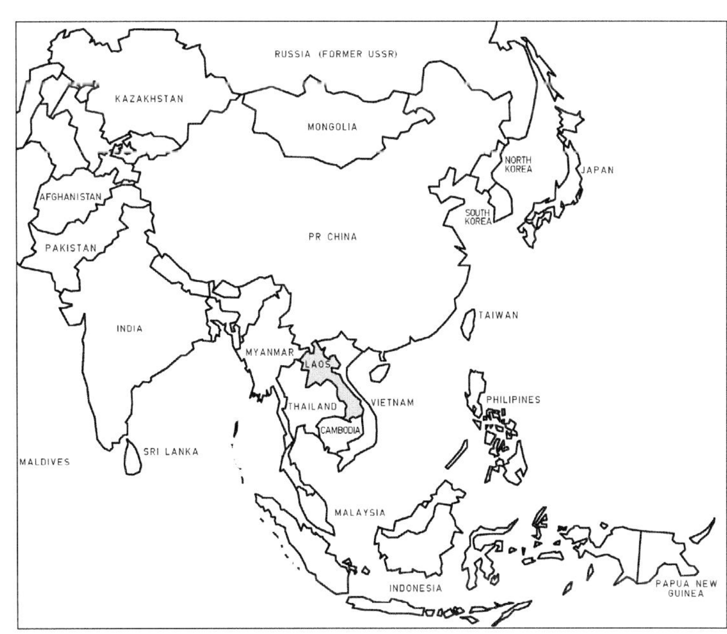

ABBREVIATIONS AND ACRONYMS

AA	Anti-Aircraft
AAA	Anti-Aircraft Artillery
AD	Auto Défense (Self Defence)
ADC	Auto Défense de Choc (Self Defence, Shock)
AFB	Air Force Base
ANL	Armée Nationale Laotienne (Laos National Army)
AVL	Aviation Laotienne (Laotian Aviation)
ARVN	Army of the Republic of Vietnam
BC	Bataillon Commando (Commando Battalion)
BCL	Bataillon Chasseur Laotien (Laotian Chasseur Battalion)
BP	Bataillon Parachutiste (Parachute Battalion)
BI	Bataillon d'Infanterie (Infantry Battalion)
BIL	Bataillon d'Infanterie Laotienne (Laotian Infantry Battalion)
BS	Bataillon Spécial (Special Battalion)
BV	Bataillon Volontaire (Volunteer Battalion)
Brig Gen	Brigadier General
CAT	Civil Air Transport
CCEC	Counter Coup d'État Committee
CIA	Central Intelligence Agency
C-in-C	Chief-in-Command
CO	Commanding Officer
Col	Colonel
COSVN	Central Office for South Vietnam
DMZ	Demilitarised Zone (Dividing North and South Vietnam)
DNC	Directorate of National Coordination
ECCOIL	Eastern Construction Company in Laos
FAL	Forces Armées Laotiennes (Laotian Armed Forces)
FAN	Forces Armées Neutralistes (Laotian Neutralist Forces)
FAR	Forces Armées Royales (Royal Armed Forces, Laos Government)
Gen	General
GM	Groupement Mobile (Mobile Group)
GMS	Groupement Mobile Spécial (Special Mobile Group)
GT	Groupement Tactique (Tactical group)
HQ	Headquarters
JUSMAG	Joint US Military Assistance Group Thailand
Lt	Lieutenant
Lt Col	Lieutenant-Colonel
1st Lt	First Lieutenant
2nd Lt	Second Lieutenant
MAAG	Military Assistance and Advisory Group
Maj	Major
MMF/GRL	Mission Militaire Française près du Gouvernement Royal du Laos
MMFI/GRL	Mission Militaire Française d'Instruction près du Gouvernement Royal du Laos
MR	Military Region
NCO	Non-commissioned officer
PARU	Police Aerial Reinforcement Unit
PAVN	People's Army of Vietnam
PEO	Program Evaluation Office
PL	Pathet Lao
RAF	Royal Air Force
RAAF	Royal Australian Air Force
RM	Région Militaire (Military Region)
RNZAF	Royal New Zealand Air Force
RTA	Royal Thai Army
RTAF	Royal Thai Air Force
SEATO	South East Asia Treaty Organization
SGU	Special Guerrilla Unit
USMC	United States Marine Corps
USOM	United States Operations Mission
USAF	United States Air Force
USN	United States Navy
VNAF	Vietnam Air Force
VPAF	Vietnam People's Air Force

ACKNOWLEDGMENTS

The authors wish to express their special gratitude to all those individuals who contributed to this book. Specifically, we wish to express our deepest appreciation to André Gillard, Anthony J. Tambini, Chau Huu Loc, Dang Huy Lang, Do Khac Mai, Ha Minh Tay, Ho Dac Du, Ha Mai Viet, Huynh Sanh Thong, Huynh Ba Phuc, Huynh Thu Thoai, Jean Dunoyer, Ken Conboy, Le Quang Thuan, Le Xuan Lan, Mai Van Hai, Nguyen Tien Van, Nguyen Xuan Giac, Pham Long Suu, Pham Quang Khiem, Philippe Charton, Robert C. Mikesk, Roger Routin, Stephane Legoff, Ted Koppel, Terry Love, Timothy Keer, Timothy Pham, Tom Cooper, Tran Tan Tiep, Ung Buu Hoang Nguyen, Vo Ngoc Cac, and Vu Dinh.

All of them provided extensive aid in one form of related research or the other, helping to make this book possible.

PROLOGUE

The 'Vietnam War' is generally regarded as a clash in South Vietnam between the United States and North Vietnam; actually, this was already the second such conflict in succession in the region, and it extended well into most of Southeast Asia, including Laos, Cambodia and even into Thailand.

Washington's policy was driven by China's fall to the Communists in 1949 and fear Beijing (Peking) would ultimately control all of Southeast Asia, with the countries falling one-by-one like a line of dominoes.[1] These fears became more acute with the outbreak of the Korean War in 1950, leading the Americans to reverse their traditional anti-colonialist policies in Indochina of five years earlier. As a result, the Americans provided the French with massive military and economic aid and, in one form or another, this policy continued with the former French colonies until 1972, when the normalisation of relationships saw Washington withdraw from the region within three years.

The escalating conflict in Vietnam soon spread to its neighbours, Cambodia, and Laos, while Thailand became a rear base for the United States war effort. This mini-series will focus on this 'out-country' aspect of the conflict, with this first volume describing the events in Laos, Vietnam's first unfortunate neighbour to be caught in a very destructive war.

The Laos conflict is often portrayed as a deluge of bombs falling on simple people living centuries-old ways of life. Much of this is propaganda but it has a kernel of truth. More than 2 million tonnes of bombs did fall on Laos and to this day the central Plain of Jars is as cratered as the surface of the Moon. But, this represents only part of the picture of a multi-layered and complex conflict.

At the domestic level a dynamic, modern, nationalist, revolutionary movement, the Pathet Lao (Land of the Lao), sought to overthrow the kingdom's centuries-old status quo and establish a single socialist nation based upon Marxist-Leninist principles, or Communism. The status quo was represented by the royal government in Vientiane, whose Francophile leadership had the technical trappings of the 20th century but whose rule owed less to the ideals of the French republic and more those of the Ancien Régime of the 18th century monarchy. Both were dependent upon external support for their success, and even survival, and here the conflict assumed a regional aspect.

Thailand, the only Southeast Asian nation successfully to resist Western colonialism and imperialism, had no desire to see either threatened by potential Communist enemies in the east, and regarded Communist China as the ultimate threat. The more immediate one was Thailand's traditional regional foe: the Vietnamese, the two competing for control of Indochina with Laos and Cambodia being alternatively occupied or forced to recognise their neighbours' suzerainty, or at best becoming buffer zones. After the French ceded independence to their Indochinese territories, Bangkok feared that Communist North Vietnam would seek to export the revolution directly, or indirectly, into Laos and Cambodia, especially if it won the struggle for non-Communist South Vietnam. There was a personal element for Bangkok, for not only were the lowland Laotians cousins of the Thais, but also there were five times more of them in Thailand than on the opposite bank of the Mekong. Thailand reacted to Hanoi's actions by dispatching troops into South Vietnam and Laos as well as hosting American airbases, leading both North Vietnam and China to support communist insurgency in Thailand.

For their part, Cambodia and Laos sought to safeguard their territories and avoid entanglement in South Vietnam's developing

Even today, many parts of the Laotian countryside remain pock-marked with bomb craters. Since 1975 it is estimated more than 20,000 civilians have been killed or injured when they came into contact with unexploded bombs. (Philippe Charton)

Despite the upheaval provoked by the Second World War and the French Indochina War in political, social and cultural fields, Laos was still a traditional society by mid-1950s which remained very attached to the monarchical system. The Royal Ballet troupe was seen here performing in front of the royal place in Luang Prabang, the Phra-Lak Phra-Lam, the Lao version of the sacred poem, the Ramayana. (Albert Grandolini Collection)

conflict. But, their fragmented elites steered their countries into the conflict, partly because the North Vietnamese sought to extend their influence and power within both countries, acting like former Vietnamese emperors, essentially establishing protectorates in eastern Laos and Cambodia in their pursuit of victory in South Vietnam.

In seeking to prop up the Southeast Asian 'dominoes', the United States became committed to a proxy war in Laos, partly to shield Thailand and partly to stop the perceived Communist threat. Military operations in Laos were regarded as secondary to the struggle in South Vietnam, with Washington's hands tied by international agreements guaranteeing the independence of Laos and Cambodia, leaving covert military operations and aerial bombardment the only means of confronting Hanoi.

Ultimately, everything depended upon the North Vietnamese and from the start the attitude of Hanoi towards the agreements it signed over the future of Laos and Cambodia was 'Who compels us to keep the promises we make?' Vietnamese cadres (organisers) have written memoirs of their activities in both countries: 'What comes through clearly in these accounts is the degree to which these communists believed in their missions in Laos, the righteousness of the cause, its legitimacy and their duty to spread the revolutionary word there'.[2] This single-minded determination would drive Hanoi to ultimate victory, as it sought within both Laos and Cambodia a mirror image of its own socio-economic revolution.

1

SHAPING THE COCKPIT

Laos is a land-locked country of 236,800 square kilometres in Southeast Asia, sharing a 416-kilometre frontier with China, with its longest frontier in the east with a 1,957-kilometre border with Vietnam. The Cambodia border in the south is 492 kilometres long, while to the west lies the 1,730 kilometres of the kilometre wide Mekong River (Nam Mekong) upon whose banks lies the capital, Vientiane.

The Mekong rises in northern Laos and runs west then south to provide a second, 230-kilometre border with Shan State in Burma (Myanmar from 1989), and then establishes the border with Thailand (as Siam was renamed on 23 June 1939). The country's shape resembles a pan, and the southern half, which is some 120-240 kilometres wide, was dubbed The Panhandle by the Americans and this term will be used in future. This part of the country has numerous rivers and streams which cut deep ravines, but there are broad valleys east of Thakhek in Khammoane (now Khammouan) province, and the eastern subsidiaries of the Mekong; the Doue running through Khong Sedone and the Sau from Attopeu (now Attapu) into the low-lying terrain of Champassak, Sedone and Sithandone Provinces (Champassak has now absorbed the other provinces).

Most of the country is a thousand metres above sea level in terrain consisting largely of rugged mountains, many over 1,500 metres tall, with dense rain forests on their lower slopes and pine forests over the 1,000-metre line, the heights being quite cold. Most of the eastern frontier, which was also the provincial boundary of Phong Saly, Houa Phan, Xieng Khouang, Khammouane, Savanakhet, Saravane (now Salavan and Xe Kong provinces) and Attopeu, runs along the 1,100 kilometre long, 130-kilometre-wide Annamite Mountain Range (Day Truong Son in Vietnamese), which is 900-2,600 metres high and runs roughly parallel to the Vietnamese coast before curving into northern Cambodia. There are a few routes eastward and these exploit the handful of passes, notably the Napé and Mu Gia. The eastern, Vietnamese, slope is noticeably steeper than the western (Laotian) one and broken by numerous rivers and streams flowing eastward. The northwestern frontier runs through the Luang Prabang mountains running north-south and reaching into Thailand, with the most prominent peaks, the rugged terrain restricting major roads to just one from the provincial capital, Sainyabuli, to Thailand.

The mountains lead to two plateaux: the Xieng Khouang in the north and the Boloven (today Bolaven) in the south. The former averages 1,300 metres above sea level, and is covered by lush vegetation with numerous rivers, streams and waterfalls in a rugged karst landscape dotted with caves. It covers Luang Prabang, Houa Phan and Xieng Khouang Provinces and opens out into the Plain of Jars (Thong Hai Hin), which is some 15 kilometres wide and features thousands of pre-historic pot-like monoliths at 90 sites. This is the largest area of grasslands in northern Laos and, therefore, a major crossroads site surrounded by spectacular heavily forested limestone escarpments. The Boloven Plateau is 1,000-1,350 metres above sea level, and covers the country's four of the southern provinces of Saravane, Attopeu, Sedone and Champassak and is crossed by several rivers while featuring many waterfalls.

A mid-1960s aerial view of Vientiane. The capital of Laos laid on the eastern bank of the Mekong River, the other bank delineating the border with Thailand. (Albert Grandolini Collection)

A typical aerial view of the northeastern part of Laos with its rugged mountains that made any displacements difficult. The Royal Laotian forces deployed within these areas relied almost exclusively upon air transport. (Albert Grandolini Collection)

The country has a tropical climate influenced by monsoons, with the rainy season from May to November, and with March and April generally being the hottest months of the year. The heights of the Annamites can suffer fierce monsoon rains of up to 200 millilitres per year, but on the western slopes the monsoon alternates with the hot, dry, 'Lao wind'. While the fighting grew in scale the country's population grew from nearly 1.9 million in 1955 to 2.3 million a decade later and 3 million in 1975. Around 90 per cent were peasants, most of them short, around 1.65 metres (5ft 5in), and largely illiterate, with a profound reluctance to accept change even if this meant improving conditions, but starvation appears to have been unknown. There were four main ethnic groups; the Lowland Lao (Lao Loum), the Midland Lao or Lao Theung and the Highland Lao (Lao Soung) or Highlanders, and the Tai. The Lowland Lao are ethnic Laotians, Buddhists who lived predominantly in the fertile lowlands as subsistence farmers disdaining the minorities and highlanders.

The French regarded the Lowland Lao, most of whom lived in villages, as affable and charming, but indolent, with women performing most of the physical labour. Within the Highlanders the largest group, who arrived from southern China in the 19th century, were the 250,000 Hmong (free people), although most are Meo (barbarian) augmented by the Kha and Yao. They were animists and some lived a nomadic slash-and-burn existence in the heights of northern Laos leaving wedge-shaped areas cleared for crops, while others cultivated terraced rice paddies on the slopes. There was an especially large concentration in Xieng Khouang province, where the Laotian kings had given them autonomy for helping to repel a Vietnamese invasion while the French allowed them to administer themselves through elected clan leaders (kiatong). The Lao Theung, often referred to as Kha (slave), were of Cambodian origin and lived on the upper slopes of the Panhandle, having traditionally been exploited by the Lowland Lao. The Tai, who spoke heir own language, lived in mountain valleys and were largely concentrated in Phong Saly, Houa Phan and Xieng Khouang provinces and were sub-divided into Black, Red and White Tai depending upon their tribal colours.

From Independence to Dependence

Modern Laos dates to the mid-14th century with the establishment of the Lan Xang kingdom, which straddled the Mekong and extended into modern China, Vietnam, Myanmar (Burma), Thailand and Cambodia. Its capital was Luang Prabang until Burmese pressure saw it moved in the mid-16th century to Vientiane (the romanised spelling of the Lao name Vieng Chan), on the banks of the Mekong. Under King Sourigna Vongsa, the kingdom reached the peak of its power during the 16th century, but from the beginning of the 18th century it split into three regional kingdoms. They were sucked into the power struggle between Burma and Siam in a kaleidoscope of ever-changing alliances, but the Siamese victory then overran southern and central Laos to make northern Laos a vassal state by 1780 and for a century afterwards large numbers of Laotians were forcibly moved west of the Mekong depopulating much of the country.[1]

The early 18th century saw Siam facing a new threat from the east, where ethnic Vietnamese steadily expanded down the coast to reach the Mekong Delta by 1760. They increased their control in the Vientiane region and across the Mekong with a surge of Vietnamese settlers. In the midst of civil war in Vietnam, Siamese troops marched into Vientiane in 1778, but during the 19th century another wave of Vietnamese refugees, mostly Catholics escaping persecution, arrived in northeast Thailand. During the 1830s the Vietnamese began to seize portions of Laotian territory, leading to two wars with Siam over both Laos and Cambodia, but Bangkok's grip on Laos steadily tightened during this period. Siam's aims were to fragment the threat posed by the Laotian princes, to ensure Bangkok's security and to

(Map by Anderson Subtil, based on Ted Hooton)

block the Vietnamese advance across the Annamite Mountains into the Mekong valley. Simultaneously, refugees including the Hmong moved into northeastern Laos to escape unrest in China.

Europeans, specifically the British and French, began exerting political influence within the region during the 19th century. The French had followed The Cross since before the Revolution in 1789 and from the mid-19th century, Paris expanded its presence in Vietnam beginning with the 1862 Treaty of Saigon, which opened the Mekong Delta to French trade. This hoped to follow the Mekong into southern China but the physical difficulties of traversing the upper reaches of the river made this impossible. In 1886 the French began developing a presence in southern Laos bringing them into conflict with the Siamese, but they gradually established a protectorate in northern Laos. They retained direct control of southern Laos, which was formally recognised following victory in the 1893 Franco-Siamese War, and the 1904 Entente Cordiale confirmed that Laos, with Cambodia, were within the French sphere of influence. The French called their new territory Laos and established its capital at Vientiane, whose population grew to some 35,000 after the Second World War, making it the country's biggest town, but Luang Prabang in the north remained the traditional royal capital.[2]

Northern Laos was regularly ransacked by Chinese bands known as the Black, Yellow, and Red Flags, who even briefly occupied Vientiane in 1874 during the Haw Wars. Siamese King Chulalongkorn decided to send troops into Laos to shield Siam from their incursions. Siamese troops are seen here entering Luang Prabang in 1888 during their second campaign in Laos. (Albert Grandolini Collection)

Despite their defeat against the French in 1893, the Siamese continued to maintain forces in Laos that regularly skirmished with the French trying to advance into Laos. This detachment of Siamese troops in Sayaboury Province prepare to finally leave Laos in 1904. (Albert Grandolini Collection)

Laotian King Sisavang Vong succeeded his father King Zakarine in April 1904. He is seen here, in 1928, with his French colonial advisers. (Albert Grandolini Collection)

Paris's rule was conducted by the Vientiane-based Résident Superieur, but French influence was extremely limited because few Europeans were willing to live there as there was little of economic value. While the French developed infrastructure, supervised trade and collected taxes, direct control of the population devolved to villages (chao muang). The Siamese depopulation of Laos, the absence of any educated Laotians and their lack of dynamism led the French to encourage Vietnamese and Chinese immigration to fill the senior and mid-level governmental positions, Laotians being confined to the lower levels, and in the major towns the Vietnamese were in the majority. Only in 1928 was the first training school established for Laotians to enter the higher levels of the bureaucracy, but indigenous attendance in secondary schools was low and even fewer went on to university. This period saw the French belatedly begin a programme of public works, notably road building, establishing basic educational and health care frameworks as the first stirrings of Laotian nationalism began, with an increased interest in national history and culture. But, while the Lao elite accepted the French view that the country needed to be modernised, there remained a fear of both the Siamese and the Vietnamese that influenced the evolution of the Indochina Communist Party (ICP) founded by Nguyen Ai Quoc, better known as Ho Chi Minh.

During 1928 he toured Laos and Siam as the clandestine East Asia Comintern delegate hosted by the Vietnamese, from whom he recruited the first communist cells, supplemented by a few Sino-Thai or Chinese immigrants living in Siam. The following year he

A group of French officers of the French Indochina Section of the SOE Force 136 gathered around an RAF Dakota in India, in spring 1945. Many of them would be parachuted into Japanese-occupied French Indochina, including Laos, to set-up resistance groups. Jean Deuve, who would lead the French DGSE Intelligence in Laos until 1963, was dropped on 29 January 1945. (Albert Grandolini Collection)

founded the Overseas Vietnamese Association for the Salvation of the Fatherland (OVASF) as an umbrella for the future ICP in both countries. After a French crackdown in Vietnam in 1930, many Vietnamese communists fled to Siam where the first Laotian ICP cells were created in Siam's Udon Province, then to the main Laotian towns, the influx helping to create the Siam Communist Party in 1934. A Laotian delegate who attended the first ICP congress, clandestinely held in Macau in March 1935, was Pham Van Xo, who was ethnically Vietnamese. In 1941, the OVASF was split into branches, for Thailand (as Siam was renamed in 1939) and Laos, covertly moving its seat from Sakhon Nakhon to Thakhet, then Vientiane, with cadres conducting propaganda and political work among the 100,000 Vietnamese living in Laos.[3]

French rule began to crumble following the outbreak of the Second World War and Germany's victory over France in 1940. The isolation of French Indochina provided Bangkok an opportunity to provoke a war which acquired some Laotian territory. Within a year, Japan occupied French Indochina, while allowing the colonial power nominal rule but with reduced status for the French colonialists. Even this fig-leaf was ripped off in March 1945 when Japan overthrew the Vichy regime and interned the colonists, although in Laos a few were able to escape to remote jungle bases and begin resistance. Under Japanese pressure, on 8 April 1945 King Sisavang Vong declared Laos an independent and unified country, with the merger of the kingdom of Luang Prabang, in the north, and the kingdom of Champassak, in the south under Prince Boun Oum, although in reality it simply passed from being a French protectorate to a Japanese one. The independence movements, which had grown from the late 1930s, now merged to form a government under Prince Phetsarath Rattanavongsa as the Lao Issara (Free Lao) movement.

War to war

'Independence' lasted barely four months, for on 15 August 1945, Japan surrendered and, knowing this heralded the return of French colonial power, Francophile elements within Laos persuaded the King to dismiss Phetsarath. Within a month the prince turned the tables leaving the monarch and royal family under house arrest and, on 12 October, the Lao Issara proclaimed an independent government. In the immediate post-war period, northern Indochina was occupied by the Chinese who grudgingly recognised French authority, and southern Indochina by the British who did so on behalf of Paris. This strengthened the hands of the Lao Issara whose more radical members established a provisional government of the Pathet Lao, whose leaders included Phetsarath's French-educated younger brother Prince Souvanna Phouma and youngest half-brother Prince Souphanouvong.

After the Japanese capitulation, Souphanouvong flew to Hanoi on 4 September, in an Office of Strategic Services (OSS) aircraft, and met Ho Chi Minh (The OSS was the wartime predecessor of the CIA). At that time Washington was supporting indigenous nationalist movements and, like many of the Lao Issara movement, Souphanouvong made common cause with the Viet Nam Doc Lap Dong Minh (League for the Independence of Vietnam) or Viet Minh, a coalition of Vietnamese nationalist groups dominated and controlled by the ICP. Souphanouvong, acting as Lao Issara Foreign and Defence Minister, helped draft an agreement in which the Lao Issara allied themselves with the Viet Minh. Knowing the weakness of the Laotian nationalist forces, Souphanouvong relied upon the Laotian ICP cells as the nucleus for Lao Issara forces. At the end of Second World War, the Vietnamese cells in Thailand also benefitted from support of the clandestine OSS-supported Free Thai movement, while the nominally pro-Japanese government in Bangkok turned a blind eye to their activities.

Ho Chi Minh's Viet Minh Government recognised the Lao Issara Government on 14 October 1945, followed by the Laos-Vietnam Mutual Assistance Treaty and the Laos-Vietnam Joint Forces Organisation. The first Lao Issara forces were organised, aided by Viet Minh cadres under Vu Huu Binh, and later became the Joint

On 17 October 1945, the Chinese troops of the 93rd Division, part of the Nationalist China occupation force of Northern French Indochina, entered Luang Prabang. (Albert Grandolini Collection)

After the capitulation of Japan, the Lao Issara Government proclaimed Laos's independence and repudiated all the treaties signed with France. Standing, fourth from right, is its leader, Prince Phetsarath Rattanavongsa. Third from right is his brother Prince Souvanna Phouma. Third from left is his half-brother, Prince Souphanouvong. This picture was taken in Thailand where the Lao Issara Government sought refuge in 1946. (Albert Grandolini Collection)

Souphanouvong, acting as the Lao Issara Foreign and Defence Minister, flew to Hanoi on 4 September 1945, to sign a Laos-Vietnam Mutual Assistance Treaty between his government and that of the Viet Minh. They also agreed to set-up a Laos-Vietnam Joint Forces Organisation and a Joint Lao-Vietnamese Army. Souphanouvong is seen here with the president of the Democratic Republic of Vietnam, Ho Chi Minh. (Albert Grandolini Collection)

Lao-Vietnamese Army. Using as its cadre the Lao Vietnamese Youth Association, an ICP-affiliated organisation, company-sized units were created with captured Japanese weapons. At Vientiane, six companies each of 100 men were formed, half of them Vietnamese and the remainder of Laotians, with one company of Thai-based Laotians. Savannakhet had two companies of Laotians, Tahkhek hosted four companies of 200 men each, half of them Vietnamese. The town also held the Lao Issara military headquarters under Souphanouvong and his deputies, Oun Sananikone and the Vietnamese Nguyen Chanh. Companies and platoons were also created in Luang Prabang, Muong Phine, Tchepone, and Lao Bao on the Vietnamese border along Route 9, while training centres were set up at Tahkhek and Savannakhet to train officers. Clearly, these forces were incapable of opposing the returning French forces who defeated them in March 1946 and re-occupied Vientiane on April 24.[4]

The Lao Issara government and troops fragmented, with most fleeing into Thailand to settle in camps that also hosted some 50,000 Vietnamese refugees fleeing northern Vietnam from the returning French forces. Thailand, under Premier Pridi Phanomyong's government, supplied some military aid to the Viet Minh and permitted Lao Issara radicals to stage some desultory, and ineffective, forays across the Mekong River, although these never posed a serious threat to the French. The fate of the Lao Issara resistance was sealed when former dictator, Field Marshal Plaek Phibunsongkhram, took power in Bangkok following an

A group of Lao Issara fighters being trained at Savannakhet in early 1946. As with the other Lao Issara armed units, most of them were recruited among the Vietnamese community living in Laos. (Albert Grandolini Collection)

The French reconquest of Laos started in December 1945, with a motorised task force of 3,200 men, organised around the 5th Colonial Infantry Regiment, advancing from Hue in Vietnam along Colonial Route 9, with air support. (André Gillard Collection)

The new strongman in Bangkok, Plaek Phibunsongkhram quickly launched a crackdown on the Lao Issara. The survivors relied now on the Vietnamese Viet Minh to restructure the movement into the Communist Pathet Lao. (Albert Grandolini Collection)

In order to reinforce the Lao Issara forces in southern Laos, the PAVN sent reinforcements from Vietnam along Colonial Route 9 to Savannakhet at the end of 1945. It was the first time that the PAVN intervened directly into Laos. (PAVN)

As in northern Vietnam, the Nationalist Chinese reluctantly withdrew from Laos after protracted negotiations. These Nationalist Chinese troops are departing Vientiane and transiting through Tchepone. As with most units deployed in northern French Indochina, they boarded ships in Haiphong Harbour to be redeployed in Manchuria to confront the Chinese communist advance. (André Gillard Collection)

Tanks in the streets of Bangkok, a regular occurrence in Thailand's eventful contemporaneous political history. These Japanese-built Type 95 light tanks participated in the November 1947 coup that brought back to power Field Marshal Plaek Phibunsongkhram, who had allied his country with Japan during the Second World War. He made Thailand a bastion of anti-communism in Southeast Asia with the support of Washington. (Albert Grandolini Collection)

Army coup in November 1947. The anti-Communist leader began a rapprochement with France, ending military aid to the Viet Minh and cracking-down upon the Lao Issara, whose last cross-river attack around Pakse was in February 1950. These guerrillas were encircled and destroyed by a rising star of the new French sponsored Laotian national army, Lieutenant Phoumi Nosavan, himself a former Lao Issara officer.[5]

Viet Minh resistance showed the French the clock could not be fully turned back, and in August 1946 Paris made Laos a constitutional monarchy, with the elected Vientiane-based government controlling domestic affairs. Although the French retained key administrative and military positions, and Paris continued to direct foreign policy and defence, its grip on the country began to ease. The more moderate and conservative elements of the Lao Issara, including Souvanna Phouma, returned and competed in the first national elections in March 1947, while some Lao Issara officers were offered assignments in the French-sponsored local units. The election was less a contest between political ideologies and more of a contest between a score of largely aristocratic families or clans representing personal and regional interests, and this would bedevil Laotian politics until the 1975 Revolution. Nevertheless, the constitution it promulgated in May 1947 made the country an independent state within the French Union.

The Franco-Lao General Convention of 19 July 1949 gave the Laotians a greater say in foreign affairs, and the transfer of power accelerated. The Lao Issara movement was now redundant and dissolved itself in October 1949, having achieved most of its aims with many of its members creating the National Progressive Party (Phak Sat Kao Na) under Souvanna Phouma. There was now steady progress from autonomy to independence, and on 6 February 1950 Paris transferred almost all its powers to an independent Laos, which was promptly recognised by the United States, Great Britain and in Thailand, where Phetsarath's policy was to remain neutral in the growing Cold War between the Communist and Capitalist worlds. Total independence was finally obtained through the Franco-Lao Treaty of Amity and Association of 22 October 1953. Independence also saw the creation on 1 July 1949 of the Armée Nationale Laotienne (ANL), at a time when the military situation was approaching crisis point for the French, who faced outright war from 1946 with the prime fronts in Tonkin and central Vietnam (Annam).

Meanwhile, Souphanouvong, accompanied by Thao O. Anourack, sought help in Tonkin, increasingly controlled by the Viet Minh, allowing Ho Chi Minh to demand independence for all French Indochina's nations. Laos proved very important to the Viet Minh by providing their forces in Tonkin room for manoeuvre, although they had few resources to share with their Laotian comrades, yet some arms were smuggled across the country's long and poorly patrolled border. Arms also came from the Burmese and Thai governments until 1947, then increasingly from China.[6] Souphanouvong reorganised bands of Hmong guerrillas, under Lo Phung Pablia, Xieng Sinh and Faydang Blia Yao, around Son La and Dien Bien Phu, from where they launched forays into northeastern Laos. But, the foundation of a Laotian communist army came from the remnants of the Lao Issara forces under their

Eastern Committee. This was led by Vietnamese Viet Minh leader, and former trader, Nouhak Phoumsavan and a Vietnamese-Laotian Communist lawyer, Kaysone Phomvihane, both of whom were members of the ICP, which was ostensibly disbanded in November 1945. Together they reorganised the Laotian forces and Kaysone led the first 300 fighters, the Latsavong Detachment, across the Vietnamese border.[7]

To lay the foundation of a Pathet Lao political organisation, the Viet Minh despatched 500 cadres into Laos at the end of 1946, another 200 arriving the following year, Nouhak being in charge of directing supporting operations from a base at Con Cuong in Tonkin.[8] For most of the Indochina War, the Pathet Lao forces remained an extension of the Viet Minh, under the direct command of their War Inter Zone-4, covering central Vietnam, although in early 1947, the Viet Minh's General Association of Overseas Vietnamese for National Salvation decided to establish the Laos-Cambodia, later Western Front, under Colonel Vu Huu Binh. In July 1948, a Special Laos Sub-Zone was created under Colonel Tran Cong Khanh at Ta Ngo, just across the Vietnamese border. Several months later, the Western Front was reorganised into four sectors: Special Zone 1 covered Vientiane, Special Zone 2 around Tahkhek, Special Zone 3 in the Savannakhet area and Special Zone 4 covering Battambang in northern Cambodia, their prime activities being infiltration of armed propaganda teams and staging the occasional ambush.[9]

The Viet Minh created a Lao front organisation, the Lao People's Progressive Organisation, in February 1949 under Souphanouvong who, while nominally remaining in Lao Issara steadily moved Leftwards. To support the expansion of Pathet Lao power, the Viet Minh began organising Team 210 to maintain a secure route from Tonkin through Laos into northern Thailand, to protect the movement of cadres. Team 219 operated east of Vientiane, while Team 9 launched armed propaganda operations in Xieng Khouang Province, being expanded in 1948 into the 210th, 215th, and 219th Companies. That year also saw the 74th Company operating in Houa Phan Province (often called Sam Nuea after the provincial capital), supported by Viet Minh's Vietnam-based Inter-Zone 3 while, Inter-Zone 4 deployed Hmong guerrillas of the 265th Battalion to harass the traffic along Route 7.

Recruiting Montagnard tribesmen became a priority, with the creation on 16 May 1948 of the Northern Laos Committee covering northwest Laos as well as the Muong Sing area. A training camp was established for Lu tribesmen inside Burma across the Mekong River at Pa Leo, but transferred some months later to Muong Xa in Laos, while in early 1949 the Viet Minh 910th Battalion was given a temporary assignment to train Lu, Akha and Black Tai tribesmen.[10] The rugged mountains of Northern Laos were targeted not only due to the limited French administrative presence but also because Montagnards grew opium there, and this provided both the Laotian and Vietnamese Communists a revenue source to finance their war effort with the insurgency surging during the opium-harvesting season. For example, during 1950, the People's Army of Vietnam (PAVN), or Quan Doi Nhan Dan Viet Nam, dispatched the 532nd and 910th Battalions of the 138th Regiment to protect the drug caravans reinforced by two companies of the 77th Regiment.[11]

In rural areas and among ethnic minorities, the Viet Minh sent in armed propaganda teams to organise militias and guerrilla groups. For a long time, they were only poorly armed, with spears, crossbows and flintlocks, like this detachment in Xieng Khouang Province in 1946. (PAVN)

An officer addresses troops of the Viet Minh War Inter Zone-4 in 1947. This command controlled operations in an area which straddled central Vietnam and southern Laos. (PAVN)

By the early 1950s, the ANL had been steadily expanded from some 4,000 men to 15,000, with six infantry and six light infantry battalions, augmented by eight provincial internal security battalions and an elite paratrooper battalion. The pennants of these units were officially presented during the That Luang religious festival in honour of the great yellow stupa of Vientiane in November 1953. (ECPA)

2

LAOS BECOMES A BATTLEGROUND

By early 1950, the Pathet Lao were also infiltrating into southern Laos, creating the Lower Laos Resistance Zone under Khamtay Siphandone, with Sithon Kommadam as his deputy for military affairs. The effort began modestly with the arrival in the Saravane area of 100 Pathet Lao guerrillas, mostly ethnic Vietnamese from Thailand, supported by the 44th and 200th PAVN Companies, but, within a year, guerrillas were operating in the Boloven Plateau around Attopeu, while the 64th and 364th PAVN Battalions staged occasional cross-border ambushes and raids. Later a permanent PAVN unit, the battalion-sized Group 280, was formed from the former 6th, 75th, and 77th Companies to operate along Route 12, while the 364th PAVN Battalion, later renamed the 1st Battalion, operated along the southern part of Route 9.[1]

The struggle within Laos remained at a very low level, the Pathet Lao/Viet Minh concentrated upon tightening their control of the Annamite Mountain area, with cadres organising remote villages by improving everyday life through revolutionary nationalism with little reference to Marxism. In August 1950, Souphanouvong held a meeting that established the Neo Lao Issara (Free Laos Front) as a political umbrella and a revolutionary government with himself as President and Foreign Minister, Kaysone as Defence Minister and Nouhak as Finance Minister. This triumvirate would be the heart of the Lao revolutionary government until it achieved power in 1975, and the meeting defined the political strategy as well as 'the nature and extent of its dependency on the Communist Vietnamese for ideological, organisational and logistic support'.[2] The Pathet Lao Government installed itself in Tonkin, in Thanh Hoa Province, before moving to Phu Quy in Nhe An Province in 1952. The new movement sought to mobilise the minorities such as the Hmong in the north and the Kha on the Boloven Plateau, where the writ of central government had rarely been strong and was intrusive, for example through collecting taxes. Unlike the Viet Minh, however, the Pathet Lao did not establish autonomous areas for the minorities although they offered them a role in developing the new nation as true Lao patriots.[3]

Fighting increases in Laos

To extend control, the Viet Minh despatched another 5,000, largely Vietnamese, cadres into Laos during 1950 as well as extending control along the northern Annamite Mountains, the southern Bolovens Plateau and also north of the Plain of Jars. The PAVN units operating inside Laos were now regrouped within a Vietnamese Volunteer Army commanded by Colonel Ta Xuan Thu, with the battalion-sized groups operating within specific provinces; Group 81 in Xieng Khouang, Group 82 in Luang Prabang and Huoi Xai, Group 83 in Vientiane and the two southernmost districts of Luang Prabang, and Group 280 in Hua Phan and Phong Saly. The French responded at the end of 1951 by launching a series of operations in northern Laos which dispersed the PAVN forces.[4]

The lowland Laotian population, influenced by the royal capital of Luang Prabang, remained firmly under Vientiane's control and were profoundly distrustful of the Vietnamese-dominated Viet Minh. In August 1951 the Progressives won 15 of the 39 seats, the Voravong clan's Democratic Party (Prasathipatay) led by Kou Voravong and his brother-in-law Major Phoumi Nosavan, won four, while Bong Souvannavong's National Lao Union (Lao Rouam Samphan) won three, the remaining 17 going to independents. Souvanna Phouma formed his first government, yet the elite made no effort to create a national identity and largely ignored the minorities. A French advisor noted that, as with France's Ancien Régime: 'There was too much corruption, too many favours and unfair promotions, too much supremacy of personal over national interests'.[5] This distrust of the Vietnamese extended into Cambodia and created the potential for a strong political opposition to the Viet Minh and the ICP, especially as from 1948 the French sought political allies by giving autonomy to their former colonies and protectorates.

Ho Chi Minh and the Viet Minh leadership recognised they needed to make major political changes. Although the ICP was formally disbanded in February 1951, it decided at its Second Congress to create three, autonomous nationally based Communist parties, less to direct the anti-imperialist struggle and more to lay the foundations for social-economic revolution and ultimately to create an Indochina federation. The Laotian element, which became the Lao People's Party (Phak Paksakson Lao), had 2,100 members of whom all but 31 were Vietnamese. Members of the Vietnamese Communist Party (now called the Vietnamese Workers' Party or Dan Lao Dong) were assured 'the Vietnamese Party reserves the right to supervise the activities of its brother parties in Cambodia and Laos'.[6] But recruiting for the new parties was slow, and by 1952 there were only 433 Laotian members, indeed recruitment difficulties meant the Lao People's Party (Phak Paksakson Lao) would not be formed until 22 March 1955, and be renamed the Lao People's Revolutionary Party (Choummali Saignason) in 1972. Creating autonomous Pathet Lao military units also made glacial progress; in 1951 PAVN trained 18 classes of Pathet Lao guerrillas and three officers' classes, but a more intense effort the following year saw the creation of some 120 Pathet Lao groups of around 10 men each, together with two companies and four platoons of part-time guerrillas as well as two companies of 'regular troops'.[7]

By 1953 the war was reaching a crisis point, as PAVN steadily expanded and by mid-year had an estimated 200,000 strong main and local force and a further 150,000 in self-defence groups. It was steadily improving in capability, aided by substantial military supplies and advisors from Communist China.[8] The bulk of these forces consisted of militia-type self-defence forces (Tu Ve) which operated around their villages and conducted low-level insurgency operations supporting the local forces (Dia Phuong), which conducted major operations at regional level, such as assaulting positions and ambushing convoys. At the top was the field army (Chu Luc), whose spearhead were highly mobile divisional light infantry formations, also called Main Force units, capable of roaming great distances and conducting major offensive operations.

The priority of France's Fourth Republic, established on 27 October 1946, was to rebuild a nation badly battered by the Second World War, a task in which it largely succeeded. But, this restricted resources available to fight major colonial wars, especially Marxist-influenced insurgencies; indeed the conflict in Algeria played a major part in the republic's fall. Consequently, the strength of the French

Far-Eastern Expeditionary Corps (Corps Expéditionnaire Français en Extrême-Orient: CEFEO) dropped between 1952 and 1953 from 201,000 to 190,000 soldiers, sailors and airmen, with the military burden placed largely upon the famed Foreign Legion (Légion étrangère) and the French Union's overseas territories themselves, often based upon ad hoc battalions (bataillons de marche) on two-to-five-year tours.

By the beginning of 1954, the CEFEO had 245,000 troops, of whom 177,000 were ground troops, reflecting a major expansion of indigenous forces within Indochina. They now provided a third of its strength, including 46 infantry battalions of which 36 were Vietnamese, while Metropolitan forces provided a quarter. This figure excluded militia forces similar to those of the Viet Minh and a substantial force of 8,500 indigenous (autochtones), and from the highlanders, with another 13,500 in the regular forces including separate battalions.[9]

The foundation of the CEFEO were its French Metropolitan and colonial infantry battalions, of which there were 80, including elite paratroopers, at the beginning of 1954, many confined to specific sectors on defensive duties, with 75-80 percent in Tonkin. Some were organised into mobile groups (groupes mobiles), a dozen in Tonkin, which were motor/mechanised regimental-sized formations, often including some of the dozen elite paratrooper battalions, acting as reaction forces or spearheading offensive operations.

Indigenous forces increasingly replaced the French in the static defence role, but the dominant Vietnamese forces adopted a more dynamic role with their own mobile groups, while there were also one or two highlander groups. The creation of the ANL was as much a reflection of France's declining military position as a commitment to Laotian independence, for it continued to operate under Land Forces, Laos (Forces Terrestres du Laos – FTL) command. At the time of Laotian independence, the ANL had some 4,000 men organised into four infantry battalions (Bataillon d'Infanterie Laotiennes – BIL) and a paratrooper battalion (Bataillon Parachutiste Laotien 1 – BPL1), augmented by eight provincial internal security battalions (Bataillons Chasseurs Laotiens), most in northern and central Laos but with two in the Panhandle, as well as support units. In 1953 the ANL was further expanded to some 15,000, with two infantry and six light infantry battalions (Bataillons Léger Laotiens), each no more than 300 men, for static defence while a light armoured reconnaissance squadron was formed to cover Route 13, the country's most important road running parallel with the Mekong.

The ANL was supported by two paramilitary forces; 20 (later 40) National Guard Companies (Compagnies de la Garde Nationale-CGN) and the Mixed Airborne Commando Group (Groupe de Commandos Mixtes Aéroportés-GCMA), an irregular counter-insurgency force raised from highlanders later renamed the Mixed Intervention Group (Groupement Mixte d'Intervention-GMI). The CGN were formed from November 1950 and with 4,300 poorly trained and armed men were the equivalent to the Viet Minh/Pathet Lao self-defence forces, while the GCMA/GMI were essentially guerrillas operating in Pathet Lao/Viet Minh territory. They were formed from 1952 largely among the Hmong, who had some 2,800 men supplied by air to control large parts of Houa Phan and Phong Saly, one of the leading lights being a Hmong leader called Vang Pao. It was supervised by the 100-strong Mission Militaire Française près du Gouvernement Royal du Laos (MMF/GRL), under Major Detton Lewyeski, which had ambitious plans for a force of 23 battalions.[10]

The French Intelligence SDCE decided to arm the highlander minorities of Vietnam and Laos to create guerrilla areas behind the communist lines of communication by creating, in April 1951, the Mixed Airborne Commando Group (Groupe de Commandos Mixtes Aéroportés-GCMA), later renamed the Mixed Intervention Group (Groupement Mixte d'Intervention-GMI) in December 1953. The programme was very successful with the Hmong in Laos and a similar scheme was later adopted by the CIA. A group of Hmong troops pose before joining the 2,000 strong column of Operation D (Desperado) that tried to reach the encircled garrison of Dien Bien Phu in April 1954. (Jean Sassi Collection)

The only real reserve unit of the ANL was the 1st Bataillon Parachutiste Laotien (BPL 1), which could be inserted quickly into a threatened area. The unit was created in October 1951 and thereafter was engaged in most of the operations carried out against the Viet Minh in Laos. (ECPA)

The SDCE used a small number of civilian registered aircraft, including DHC-2 Beavers and C-47s, to support its different GCMA units. (André Gillard Collection)

Success for PAVN

When first tested, the new army proved a slender reed. Fighting was confined east of the Annamites, but in April 1953 the Viet Minh struck deep into Laos both to stretch the CEFEO and to strengthen the Pathet Lao who had only 2,000 troops and militia, and while only 300 joined their comrades it was the regional logistical network which proved the more valuable asset. With Communist China controlling the northern border, from 1950 military aid flowed into Tonkin permitting semi-conventional operations in the region, but provisions were difficult to move south to support operations in Annam and Cochinchina. For this the Viet Minh needed a new logistic route through the Annamite Mountains to bypass French-occupied Annam, a plan which sowed the seed for what became a decade later the Ho Chi Minh Trail.

The offensive under PAVN commander-in-chief General Vo Nguyen Giap was on three fronts and involved 10 Viet Minh regiments: six from the 304th and 308th Divisions, two from the 312th Division, the 98th Regiment of the 316th Division, and the independent 148th Regiment.[11] The main axis along Route 6 was directed personally by Giap using the 308th and 312th Divisions with the 98th Regiment to take Sam Nuea, while there was a secondary thrust into Xieng Khouang along Route 7 by 304th Division and an understrength Pathet Lao battalion. Meanwhile, the 148th Regiment staged a diversion from the Dien Bien Phu area towards Luang Prabang. The French and Laotian garrison evacuated Sam Nuea on 12 April and trekked to the Plain of Jars, while on 19 April the French also evacuated Xieng Khouang.[12] The arrival of the 148th Regiment near Luang Prabang, with the ANL troops deserting in droves, prompted the French to send in reinforcements by air to consolidate the defences of the Royal capital, but the Communists now controlled much of northwest Laos.

A substantial injection of French troops, however, many from across the Annamites but some from Cambodia, forced back the PAVN field army across the mountains, although the Viet Minh retained control of the north-eastern border provinces of Phon Saly and Houa Phan as well as the northeastern part of the Plain of Jars. In the mountains, the Viet Minh began enlarging trails, creating staging bases and moving supplies to depots in the Kontum area of Vietnam's Central Highlands. Despite the setback, the Laos campaign successfully demonstrated PAVN's ability to project military power over long distances. The Viet Minh mobilised some 35,000 porters with 2,000 bicycles and 180 pack horses to bring in more than 6,500 tonnes of food, including 3,640 cattle, over rugged terrain to support a powerful force 400 kilometres from its own depots. In part this was achieved by repairing 170 kilometres of Route 7, and the experience would later help Giap to plan his Dien Bien Phu campaign.[13] The campaign also meant Souphanouvong could move the Pathet Lao's seat of government to Sam Nuea on 19 May 1953. This was an ideal sanctuary for the Pathet Lao because it was close to the border with Tonkin with numerous limestone caves in which to hide.

Laos briefly became a military backwater, although the 22 October 1953 agreement left France with an obligation to defend the country. Paris had decided to accelerate the process of passing the burden of the conflict to the indigenous governments, and in May 1953 nominated a new Indochina commander-in-chief, Général de Corps d'Armée Henri Navarre. His mission was to gain the upper hand over the Viet Minh within 18 months and then open negotiations from a position of strength. The Navarre Plan consisted of major operations against the enemy main forces in Tonkin and central Annam, while simultaneously developing the indigenous armed forces. Giap reacted by launching diversionary offensives in northwest Tonkin, Laos and northern Cambodia to disperse the French reaction forces. He also wanted to improve and develop the new logistic corridor linking Tonkin to Cochinchina, through eastern Laos and Cambodia, to help create a liberated area south of Saigon.

On 21 December 1953, the Viet Minh launched another double thrust into Laos with the same aims as the previous year, but possibly also intending to raise revenue through the sale of the opium crop in Houa Phan and Xien Khouang Provinces. In southern Laos, PAVN attacked around Lao Bao and along Route 9, with a convoy ambushed on 16 January 1954. Another thrust against the Boloven Plateau isolated Attopeu, which was evacuated together with Lao Ngam, while many French outposts east of Paksong were also lost. On 15 January, the 101st Regiment/325th PAVN Division made a foray against Savannakhet and south of Saravane, destroying a bridge over Route 13. The French reacted by flying five battalions to their base at Seno. Throughout southern Laos, the Pathet Lao expanded their grip by recruiting among the highlander tribes. The PAVN was also very active in northern Laos with an attack by the 308th Division's 148th Regiment, supported by the Group 82 and two Pathet Lao companies.[14] On 25 January 1954, the French began to withdraw towards Muong Sai and Luang Prabang, which were reinforced by air, together with the Plain of Jars, and brought in 10 battalions of reinforcements.

The French decided this was an opportunity to cripple PAVN's Chu Luc and in March 1954 sought to achieve this by cutting the enemy supply lines at Dien Bien Phu (Meuang Thaeng), only for their foes to turn the tables upon them. As early as 6 December 1953, a special meeting of the Politburo attended by Ho Chi Minh and Giap decided to focus the PAVN main effort of the coming 1954 campaign against Dien Bien Phu, satisfied that its feint towards northern Laos would persuade the French high command to accept the town as the main battlefield in the spring. While PAVN concentrated around Dien Bien Phu it cut the garrison's communications with Laos through attacks along the Nam U River valley and along Route 13, using 7,600 troops reinforced by 10,000 Chu Luc troops. Some 300 tons of rice collected in Laos were also forwarded to Dien Bien Phu to sustain the troops, together with 400 captured 105mm artillery shells, a welcome boost for Viet Minh gunners deployed around the French base.[15]

On 7 May, the surviving French units at Dien Bien Phu surrendered and 14 irreplaceable French battalions (17 percent of those in CEFEO) were destroyed, together with a Vietnamese paratrooper unit and two Tai battalions, breaking the backbone of the CEFEO which had reduced the garrison of Tonkin's key Red River Delta from 45 to 17 battalions.[16] All prospects of winning the war had ended, indeed the second Viet Minh offensive in Laos strengthened Pathet Lao control among the minorities of central and southern Laos.

Troops from the Pathet Lao and the PAVN 304th Division pose in another staged photograph with flags of the communist Vietnamese, Laotian Pathet Lao and Cambodian Khmer Issarak movements after taking Xieng Khouang in April 1953. In reality, the Vietnamese dominated the 'alliance', relegating their allies to a role of auxiliaries. (PAVN)

Viet Minh and Pathet Lao troops come together for this propaganda photo during the PAVN multi-divisional thrust into Laos in spring 1953. (PAVN)

After losing San Nuea in April 1953 to an advance by two Viet Minh divisions, the French flew in reinforcements to create a fortified camp on the Plain of Jars. The first to land were the 800 paratroopers of the 2nd Foreign Legion Airborne Battalion (2nd BEP), loaded on 38 C-47 Dakotas. The defending forces were later augmented to six battalions supported by a dozen 105mm howitzers. (French Air Force)

In order to counter a new Viet Minh offensive against southern Laos in January 1954, the French reinforced the Seno base with four paratrooper battalions. One was the 3rd Vietnamese Paratrooper Battalion (3rd BPVN) which fought a costly battle with the elements of the PAVN 325th Division which had just taken Takhek. It suffered 390 casualties against an estimated 1,400 casualties for the Viet Minh. (ECPA)

The Geneva Conference

The Indochina War was concluding at a time when both superpowers saw the most significant changes since the end of the Second World War. For the Soviet Union the death of Stalin the previous year meant reassessing the future of World Communism, as Yugoslavia and China developed new forms of Marxist-Leninism challenging Moscow's claim to be the movement's undisputed leader.

Relations with its biggest challenger, China, were outwardly friendly but tensions were developing. For China, the end of the Indochina War provided the opportunity to lead the Third World bloc of newly independent countries created by the breaking up of Europe's empires. Beijing was especially determined to reassert its influence in Southeast Asia after a century of European intervention, but the victorious Viet Minh, who had morphed into the Tonkin-based Democratic Republic of Vietnam (DRV), claimed to represent Cambodia and Laos's 'resistance movements'.

The United States had reluctantly recognised it was in a Cold War with the communists for world leadership. Before the Second World War, Washington had little interest in Southeast Asia, but the Cold War forced a U-turn in regional diplomatic and strategic policies. On 23 December 1950, Washington signed the Pentalateral Mutual Défense Assistance Pact to provide military aid not only to France for use in Indochina but also to the three indigenous nations emerging from the French Union. At the time of Dien Bien Phu the Americans even briefly considered military intervention and, while wiser heads prevailed, the French defeat raised concern about the future.

The Americans were acutely aware the failure of their policies in China had eased the Communist take-over and were determined to prevent a repeat of those traumatic events. They were also determined to thwart any attempt by the Communists to repeat the direct aggression which opened the Korean War and, on 18 February 1954, the United States, the Soviet Union, France, Great Britain and China agreed to discuss in Geneva the consequences of both conflicts. From the opening day, on 26 April, the Geneva Conference was dominated by Indochina, indeed the first detailed discussions began on 8 May, the day after Dien Bien Phu surrendered. The participants agreed that Laos and Cambodia would become independent, and that Vietnam would be divided at the 17th Parallel with a northern entity, based upon Tonkin and a southern one based upon Cochinchina, Annam being divided between the two, and after two years there would be internationally supervised elections to decide the country's future.

Washington was aware the ICP, in whatever form, continued to dominate the Viet Minh, whose agenda called for the elimination or neutralisation of all political opponents and the consolidation of power in their hands, or those of their friends. The political structures of the three new Indochinese countries were fragile and no match for the Communists' dynamic political activity, making it likely they would quickly fall under Communist control. Washington, therefore sought some means to avoid this prospect other than military intervention. It should be noted that in a memo to the Central Intelligence Agency (CIA) Director on 9 June 1954, this idea was examined by the Board of National Estimates under Sherman Kent and rejected 'with the exception of Cambodia'. It did recognise the loss of Laos and South Vietnam would be 'profoundly damaging to the US position in the Far East in terms of national prestige'.[17]

On 16 June, the Chinese proposed the three new nations be dealt with separately, with Laos and Cambodia treated as neutral countries in the Cold War, and with foreign bases banned from their soil, a proposal backed by the Democratic Republic of Vietnam (DRV). Two days later the Viet Minh, who had anticipated their military supporters would be merged into the new nations' forces, offered to withdraw their troops from Laos and Cambodia under those conditions, having been warned at a meeting with the Soviet Union and China that otherwise it would undermine the Communist negotiating position. Reluctantly, the DRV was forced to accept this position and, with general agreement among the other participants, Beijing's suggestions were incorporated into the Geneva Accords, which also included a ceasefire, with signing completed in the early hours of 21 July. To monitor the implementation of the agreement there was to be an International Control Commission (ICC), chaired by an Indian and with Canadian and Polish members, but their decisions had to be unanimous which meant Poland could provide a Communist veto. Most of the Geneva Conference delegates also wished the ICC also to supervise Vietnam's reunification elections in July 1956, but the Viet Minh rejected this.

The only concession the French obtained was the retention in Laos of a military base at Seno, some 30 kilometres east of Savannakhet, and the maintenance of military advisory missions in both Cambodia and Laos, including up to 1,500 men in Laos. The MMF/GRL also ran the Laotian Military Academy of Chinaimo, east of Vientiane, and dispatched instructors at several various places like Seno, Pakse, and Xieng Khouang. It was supported by about a dozen aircraft, including L-20 Beavers, C-45s, C-47 Dakotas, and H-19 helicopters operating from Seno and Wattay, Vientiane's airport, which also supported ICC observers. A dedicated fleet of five Boeing 307 Stratoliners contracted from the French airline Aigle Azur Extrême-Orient, then Compagnie Internationale de Transports Civil Aériens (CITCA), provided the only direct air flights between Saigon and Hanoi, via Vientiane. In 1964 the ICC leased three of these aircraft, but on 18 October 1965 one was shot down over North Vietnam with nine ICC members. From September 1962 until June 1970, the French Air Force also provided the crews for the six white-painted UH-34 helicopters to support ICC teams. Despite their markings confusion with Air America aircraft meant their operation was increasingly hazardous, particularly over communist-controlled territory, where neither the Pathet Lao nor PAVN hesitated to fire upon them and in 1963 two damaged aircraft made forced landings and were destroyed on the ground. Thereafter, most of the remaining helicopters sustained damage from ground fire.[18]

On 21 July 1954, the signing of the Geneva Accords brought to an end the Indochina War. Both Laos and Cambodia were granted a vague neutral status. Vietnam was divided temporarily in two states until elections to be held two years later. Both South Vietnam, which opposed the partition, and United States, who did not recognise the People's Republic of China, did not sign the final protocol, dooming in the long run any real peace prospects. (VNA)

French Colonel Sore, heading the Franco-Laotian military delegation, met PAVN Colonel Dang Van Thinh of the DRV delegation at the headquarters of the ICC in Laos at Khang Khai, on 13 August 1954, for preliminary discussions about the withdrawal of Viet Minh forces from Laos. (ECPA)

The Geneva Conference created an International Control Commission (ICC) with representatives from Canada, India and Poland to supervise the cease-fire, the withdrawal of foreign forces, and the regrouping of the local forces in their assigned areas. This Indian officer has just landed at Khang Khai in August 1954. (Albert Grandolini Collection)

The French also reorganised Laotian Intelligence, with a discreet team of advisers from the French Foreign Intelligence Service (Service de Documentation Extérieure et de Contre-Espionage-SDCE) under the supervision of the Special Political Advisor to the Laotian Prime Minister. He was Jean Deuve, an experienced intelligence officer who had parachuted into Laos in January 1945 as a member of the British Special Operations Executive (SOE) to organise anti-Japanese guerrilla groups (The SOE was the British equivalent of OSS). During the Indochina War he served as the main French Intelligence officer in Laos, and in July 1955 created the Political Propaganda Special Service (Service Spécial de Propagande Politique-SSPP) attached to the Laotian Prime Minister's Office, and directed by Chao Sisouk.[19] Deuve, who remained in post until 1964, regarded the SSPP and its successors as a tool to reinforce French influence in Laos and to foster Paris's diplomatic aims based upon a Neutralist regime. By contrast Washington sought to transform Laos into an anti-communist bastion, and this created diplomatic tension between the US and France.

From October 1954 the French troops began to withdraw, the last departing on 28 April 1956, by which time the Premier of South Vietnam, Ngo Dinh Diem, announced his country would not participate in reunification elections. While the Viet Minh had withdrawn most of their troops from below the 17th Parallel, they began creating a new organisation to spearhead revolutionary war, the National Liberation Front, better known as the Viet Cong. In Laos it was the North Vietnamese and Pathet Lao whose actions began to undermine the Geneva Accords, setting the scene for new hostilities.

FRANCE'S SENO BASE

Under Article 2 of the Geneva Accords, France was allowed to retain a base in its former Indochina colonies with a garrison of up to 3,500 men. This was the Seno, or Séno, airbase, 30 kilometres east of Savannakhet at the crossroads of Routes 9 and 13, and while its name was supposed to be an acronym referring to the direction of the two runways, south-east and north-west (Sud Est-Nord Ouest-Seno), in fact they ran south-west-north-east.[20]

It dated to the Franco-Thai War of 1940-1941, but was expanded in 1947 with a surfaced runway augmented by another of steel perforated planks (PSP) to become a supply depot and military transit point able to handle some 1,500 tonnes of equipment per month to sustain a 12,000-men garrison in northern Laos for three months. The base could also accommodate up to 30 C-47s and a dozen F8F Bearcat fighters and B-26 Invader bombers and was protected by two Laotian battalions and an armoured cavalry squadron. It came into its own during the Viet Minh invasion of Laos in December 1953, when 10 battalions were flown in, making it the second largest French 'airhead' to be sustained after Dien Bien Phu.

France informed SEATO that Seno would be available in the event of a conflict with China. It featured a small Laotian garrison, while Laotian aircraft could use the facilities which the MMF/GRL also used to train Laotian airborne troops. It acted as a communications hub between Paris and French embassies in Asia, and the base was also the main French Signals Intelligence (Sigint) outpost in Asia, operated by the Army's Groupement de Contrôle Radioélectrique (GCR), jointly with the SDCE Service Technique de Recherche (STR).

The GCR/STR operated some 18 SIGINT intercept stations with 58 specialists, the antennae being installed some 5 kilometres outside. Paris had envisaged making Noumea, New Caledonia, its prime Sigint station in the Pacific Rim region, but ionospheric and meteorological conditions at Seno made it the best place to monitor radio communications throughout Southeast Asia as well as from southern China. The Americans had a very high regard for these Sigint activities, especially those covering China and North Vietnam, which the SDCE shared with the CIA and National Security Agency (NSA) under a 1953 agreement in exchange for American Sigint covering the Communist forces in eastern Europe. But budgetary constraints, and the demands for experienced troops in the growing Algerian conflict, meant Seno never achieved its authorised strength of 3,500; it had only 2,200 in 1955, 1,850 in 1956, 850 in 1957, 500 in 1958, and 462 men in 1959.

In 1959 the French Army wanted to close the base, seeing no strategic benefit remaining in Laos. But, the Foreign Ministry regarded it as France's only presence in Southeast Asia and its only SEATO asset, a view shared by the new French President, Charles de Gaulle. His policy was to confirm France as a major international power with an independent foreign policy from the two superpowers, which led him to recognise the People's Republic of China in 1964, leave SEATO on 1 July 1965, and NATO in 1967. He accelerated the development of a nuclear arsenal while retaining military bases world-wide. In Indochina, de Gaulle supported Neutralist governments in Laos, Cambodia, and even South Vietnam, which brought him into conflict with both Laotian rightist factions as well as the United States. As Laos plunged into a new civil war, Right-wing groups accused the French of siding with Souvanna Phouma and the Neutralists. Although Paris, like Washington, opposed a Communist take-over of Laos, it accepted a coalition government with Pathet Lao representatives.

Right-wing Laotians eventually forced the government formally to seek the closure of Seno which was transferred to the FAR on 26 June 1963. The Sigint installations also went, but the capability was maintained on a smaller scale with intercept stations installed inside the French ambassies in Vientiane, Bangkok, and Saigon, while a joint Franco-Cambodian Sigint station was installed in Phnom Penh. The end of Seno's eavesdropping role also marked the end of intelligence exchanges with the Americans, but the NSA quickly compensated for the loss by setting up its own Sigint intercept station at Ramasun, near Udorn in Thailand.[21]

After the states of Indochina became independent, France retained the Seno military base in southern Laos as its last military asset in Southeast Asia. The base could host some 3,500 men in addition to its airfield which could accommodate around 50 aircraft. This picture shows the airbase during the Viet Minh offensive against Savannakhet and Takhek in January 1954, when the local air group was reinforced with F8F fighters, B-26 bombers, C-47 and C-45 transports, as well as MS 500 observation aircraft. (Albert Grandolini Collection)

France maintained a mixed air group at Seno until 1963, and operated a half-a-dozen C-47s which were used to resupply the French instructor teams on the field, such as here at Xieng Khouang in May 1955, as well as supporting ICC inspecting teams. Some Dakotas wore mixed military-civilian markings which would facilitate the transit through some countries, like India, who would otherwise have forbidden military aircraft overflights without lengthy diplomatic clearances. (ECPA)

Another C-47 of the French Air Force mixed air group of Seno. It is seen here at Manila, after ferrying the French representatives during a SEATO meeting in 1958. The unit also supplied the French Military Advisory Mission in Cambodia. (Albert Grandolini Collection)

Among the aircraft based at Seno were some L-20 Beavers for liaison and medical evacuations. These aircraft wore Red Crosses for evacuating wounded French and Laotian prisoners released by the Viet Minh after August 1954 the cease-fire. (ECPA)

The L-20 Beaver was known for its short landing and take-off capabilities, but this aircraft suffered a hard landing on an improvised landing strip at Muong Peune while ferrying an ICC observer team in September 1955. French mechanics had to change the damaged wing before the aircraft could fly out. (Albert Grandolini Collection)

Up to 1958, the French Air Force 65th Helicopter Wing maintained a detachment of Sikorsky S-55s at Seno for operations in Laos. The crew of this machine check the rotor gearbox somewhere in northeastern Laos in a Hmong village in 1957. (Albert Grandolini Collection)

3

A SOLUTION, BUT NOT AN ANSWER

The Geneva Accords were all things to all men and in Laos, where an agreement ending hostilities was signed on 20 July, they failed to answer fundamental questions. In particular, that of the status of the Pathet Lao whose position was underpinned by the DRV and its strong right arm PAVN, indeed by 1954 there were 17,600 North Vietnamese troops and cadres in Laos.[1]

While the agreement foresaw the disbandment of the Pathet Lao forces, the creation of a coalition government and free elections, it temporarily granted the Pathet Lao control in the north-eastern provinces of Phong Saly and Houa Phan (often called Samneua after the provincial capital), with their government capital at Vieng Sai, while nominally under Vientiane. The provinces provided a sanctuary in which to assemble their forces that were also to be absorbed by the new Laotian government, yet the Pathet Lao, encouraged by Hanoi, regarded the territory as a base for revolutionary struggle. Vientiane's presence was nominal, with anti-Viet Minh guerrillas, including Hmong tribesmen whom Vientiane refused to withdraw, controlling only 195 of Phong Saly's 598 villages and 131 of Houa Phan's 974.

The Struggle for Phong Saly and Houa Phan

The Pathet Lao regarded themselves, and not the Royal Lao Government, as the legitimate representatives of the Lao people and had no intention of surrendering control of even a metre of 'liberated territory'. This brought the two administrations into conflict over the eastern provinces; in remote Phong Saly the government had only 400 ANL troops and Hmong guerrillas, but during the second half of the year the guerrilla force expanded to 3,000 and raided Pathet Lao positions and communications.

The Pathet Lao were determined to control Phong Saly and Houa Phan, and their 1,000 troops in the provinces were reinforced by men from the west and south by the time the Viet Minh officially withdrew on 16 October 1954.[2] Aided by advisors and instructors of PAVN's Group (Doan) 100, the Pathet Lao reorganised their troops in December 1954 regrouping all regular forces together, totalling 7,267 men, with an officer-training school along the North Vietnamese border, while a Defence Ministry was established, doubling as General Headquarters. The task was aided by experienced and well-trained cadres and one of the greatest successes was to train a small signaller force. The core consisted of the 1st, 2nd, 597th, 605th, 607th, 609th, 617th, 701st, and 705th Battalions augmented by a combat support battalion, equipped with 81mm mortars, 57mm recoilless artillery and 12.7mm anti-aircraft machine guns, a motorised transport battalion, three companies of intelligence, propaganda, and engineer troops, a security platoon, and 12 independent companies, while guerrilla and militia units brought total Pathet Lao strength to 9,138 men by January 1955.[3]

Pathet Lao troops rejoice when reunited with their comrades who had been operating in southern Laos and have now marched into their regrouping area in Houa Phan Province. (PAVN)

A Canadian officer of the ICC discusses with FAL and Pathet Lao representatives the exact positioning of their forces in Houa Phan Province in 1955. (Albert Grandolini Collection)

A main-force Pathet Lao battalion marches into their regrouping area in Houa Phan Province in 1955. (PAVN)

Souphanouvong decorates a soldier after speaking to his troops in the 'liberated Houa Phan Province' in 1955. He was determined to keep that area as a communist powerbase. (PAVN)

The Pathet Lao reinforced its regular battalions with crew-served heavy weapons, displayed here during a ceremony in 1955. They included 81mm mortars and recoilless 57mm guns. (PAVN)

In January 1955 the Pathet Lao forces clashed with the Hmong guerrillas. In Houa Phan, a largely Lowland Lao force, survivors of the GMI, continued operating west of Sam Neua at Moung Peun, while in Xieng Khouang there was a more substantial Hmong force south of the Plain of Jars. In Houa Phan, the guerrillas, redesignated Groupe Commando 3 under the ANL's Captain Sakoun Sananikone, were involved in lethal bickering throughout the first half of 1955. Vientiane ordered the Hmong guerrillas to expand their controlled areas and fighting broke out in March 1955, particularly in the southeast and northwest of Phong Saly. In June 1955 the new commander of Région Militaire 2 (RM-2), Major Sang Kittirath, moved his headquarters to Moung Peun to demonstrate Vientiane's determination to control the province and brought in BI (Bataillon d'Infanterie) 6 and 7, respectively a former regular BI and a former internal security Bataillon Chasseurs Laotienne (BCL), to strengthen security.

The Pathet Lao reacted promptly, surrounding the town with the 617th and 705th Battalions, two local companies, as well as a reinforced company of the 605th Battalion under a Frontier Security Command creating an impasse as civilian airlines and the CIA-supported airline Civil Air Transport (CAT) dropped supplies. The ANL response in July was to assemble a three-battalion relief force, assembled from RM-2, RM-3 and RM-4, while the Moung Peun garrison was reinforced by BP (Bataillon Parachutiste) 1 which, in an echo of Dien Bien Phu, was dropped by seven Dakotas, including two French and two CAT.[4] A Hmong group was encircled, then routed at Na Xala, with the Pathet Lao taking 40 prisoners, but in August the monsoon rains washed out the fighting leading to a military stalemate.[5]

The pro-government guerrillas' reported successes in Phong Saly encouraged the ANL General Staff in November 1955 to begin planning an offensive to retake both this province and Houa Phan, an idea opposed by Washington for fear it would provide the PAVN an excuse to enter the country. Interestingly, in June 1955 Thai Police General Phao Siyanon, Thailand's thuggish and corrupt Director of the Department of Administrative Intelligence with close links to the CIA, proposed sending a detachment of his para-military Border Patrol Police (BPP), the first proposal to use foreign troops in independent Laos.[6] In January 1958 an integrated political administration was created under Major Khamouane Boupha, a poorly educated but extremely effective military commander whose brother was prominent in the Pathet Lao. He was able to underpin his authority with an internal security force created from the remnants of BCL 1 and the GMI, distributed through-out the province under the headquarters of the newly created Bataillon Volontaire 11 (BV 11).[7]

Hmong guerrillas of a formerly French-created GMI unit operating in the Sam Nuea area where they harassed the Pathet Lao. (Albert Grandolini Collection)

In order to break the encirclement of Muong Peune, the ANL decided to parachute the BP 1 into the town on 7 July 1955. The troops are seen embarking in an AVRL C-47s. At that date, no Laotian crew were qualified to fly the Dakota so the mission was flown secretly by their French instructors. (Albert Grandolini Collection)

As there were not enough AVRL C-47s, the drop over Muong Peune was carried out with additional French Air Force, Civil Air Transport, and Air Laos Dakotas. One of the DC-3s of that last company is shown here with paratroopers waiting to board it. (Albert Grandolini Collection)

Shown is one of first Civil Air Transport (CAT) C-47s involved in operations in Laos which is unmarked, except for a shortened serial number on its rear fuselage. The CIA tried to keep a low profile at this date of its activities in Laos. (UTD)

Paratroopers of the BP 1 during one of the clearing operations in Houa Phan Province in 1955. Despite their efforts, the province remained firmly in communist hands. (Albert Grandolini Collection)

Lining up for battle

In the post-Geneva world, the Laotian government and its military leaders took stock. Numerically their forces were stronger than in 1954 but still depended upon 500 French officers and NCOs for technical and support expertise, yet they were due for repatriation. There was a frantic effort to train Laotian replacements, but they would take a long time to reach the French standard so there was no guarantee these forces could militarily challenge the Pathet Lao and their North Vietnamese allies waiting in the wings. The ANL, like the political establishment, was a labyrinth of internecine political intrigues in Vientiane, divided between Francophiles and nationalists, exacerbated by family rivalry and factions, all of whom were more interested in fighting each other rather than the Pathet Lao. The Army chief-of-staff was 34 years old Phoumi, who had briefly fought the French after the Second World War then joined them. Under him there were large-scale promotions, such as battalion commanders, based largely upon a mixture of family connections, seniority and even the whim of the French.

By renaming the light infantry units, the ANL now had 17 infantry battalions (bataillons d'infanterie-BI) and two paratrooper battalions (bataillon parachutiste-BP), while Lewyeski's MMF/GRL aimed to raise another four in 1955 and ultimately to absorb them into Mobile Groups (Groupes Mobiles-GM), and the strength was set at 23,500. The CGN were to be disbanded and their personnel used to create 36 company-sized commandos while the GMI, whose existence the French had denied, began to evaporate through a combination of lack of support and Pathet Lao operations. But, from June 1955 a new programme was built upon the ruins as the Auto-Défense (Self Defence) or AD, in which the ANL would use highlander battalions to strike the rear of the Pathet Lao. The irregulars were supported by the newly formed Laotian Aviation (Aviation Laotienne) created at Wattay Airfield near Vientiane on 28 January 1955, with transports and liaison aircraft and later renamed the Royal Lao Aviation (Aviation Royale Laotienne – AVRL) usually referred to by English-speaking sources as RLAF, under the Lao-Vietnamese Lieutenant Colonel Sourith Don Sasorith from 1957. To help secure the Mekong, the Laotian Navy (Marine Laotienne) was created on 28 January 1955, as part of the ANL and then became the ANL's River Flotilla (Escadrille Fluviale) with 19 small patrol boats.[8]

An ANL priority was to train sufficient officers to replace the departing French. The Chinaimo Military Academy went into an accelerated curriculum to try to graduate the required needs, and these cadets have just graduated. (Albert Grandolini Collection)

Beside the regular units, the ANL also developed local forces by merging the various within the Auto-Défense (Self-defence) militias responsible for local security. Poorly armed and mostly recruited from ethnic minorities, their combat performances varied greatly. (Albert Grandolini Collection)

The airborne component of the ANL continued to grow with two additional battalions being set up. These paratroopers of the BP 2 are seen during a parade at Luang Prabang in 1957. (Albert Grandolini Collection)

Another problem for the ANL was the transition from French weaponry, which was no longer supported, to American. That transition took nearly a decade to be completed. These female soldiers, during a parade in Vientiane, are still armed with French made MAS 38 SMGs. (Albert Grandolini Collection)

The newly created ANL infantry battalions were very unequal in their capability. They lacked supporting units and the quality of their officers and NCOs was low, and this was reflected in the field with very uneven performances. (Albert Grandolini Collection)

French combat troops left Laos by 6 August 1954, but on 28 January 1955, the French established a training facility in-country for some 200 air and ground crew, though it was clear the MMF/RLG would not remain indefinitely, and it was steadily reduced in size to meet the demands of the growing insurgency in Algeria. The MMF/GRL, renamed the Mission Militaire Française d'Instruction près du Gouvernement Royal du Laos (MMFI/GRL) in 1960, continued to decline. It was under General Jacques Lefort from September 1964 to June 1967, but by 1966 was down to 145 men; 118 attached to the army, 20 with the air force, and seven with the navy. The same year, some 74 Laotians also attended specialist courses in France, including 43 from the army, five from the Navy, and 26 from the military medical department. The last 150 French advisers departed the country only after the Communist take-over on 2 December 1975.[9] It is worth noting that radio communication in both the Laotian and Cambodian forces continued to be in French until the 1960s. With the Paris Agreement, the French announced they would cease paying the Laotian forces on New Year's Day 1955, and from October 1954 Vientiane began lobbying in Washington for US military assistance.

There was some expansion of the ANL, which by the beginning of 1956 had expanded to 23 battalions; 11 BI each with a nominal 600 men and 10 volunteer battalions (Bataillons de Volontaires-BV) for internal security with a nominal 542 men, two paratrooper battalions each with an establishment of 782 men, a third battalion being formed in early 1960 when the Airborne Command became the Airborne Regiment. They were distributed throughout the kingdom (see Table 3-1) with the largest concentration, nominally 3,000 men, in Luang Prabang. There was no formal strategic reserve, but the Laotian General Staff in Vientiane could deploy the paratrooper battalion and when a second was created in 1957 it established an Airborne Command, under the AVRL commander Colonel Sourith, which acted as such a reserve, with BP 1 at Seno supporting operations in the south and BP 2 at the Wattay Airbase (AB) for operations in the north. A single armoured reconnaissance squadron evolved into a three-squadron regiment by 1957.

Table 3-1: The ANL at the beginning of 1956

Province	Battalions
Phong Saly	BV 11
Houa Khong	BV 13
Luang Prabang	BI 1, 3, 10, 21; BV 12
Houa Phan	BI 22; BV 23
Sayaboury	BV 14
Xieng Khouang	BI 5, 25; BV 21
Vientiane	BP 2
Khammouane	BI 6; BV 31
Savannakhet	BI 12; BP 1; BV 31
Saravane/	BI 26; BV 41
Attopeu	BI 4
Sedone/ Champassak/ Sithandone/ Vapikhamtong	BV 42

The Laotian forces slowly expanded, and in July 1959 they were renamed the Forces Armées Laotiennes (Laotian Armed Forces) or FAL and were strengthened with an American-equipped 1st Artillery Group (Groupe d'Artillerie 1 -GA 1) with two batteries of M101 105mm howitzers and one battery of 4.2 inch (107mm) M2 mortars.[10] Some 15 M24 Chaffee light tanks augmented, then replaced, M5 Stuarts, together with additional M5 half-tracks. The FAL also created engineer, signals, transport, maintenance and medical support companies and military police battalions. The AVRL had eight transports; six Dakotas, two Beavers, and six L-19 Bird Dog observation aircraft with detachments scattered around the country, but the Americans were pondering providing it a light attack capability, with T-6 Texans using rifle-calibre machineguns and rockets. With the creation of the FAL the River Flotilla was upgraded to the Royal Laotian Navy (Marine Royale Laotienne-MRL), with 32 small patrol boats and landing craft but only 200 men.[11]

The prime task of the fledgeling AVRL was to provide liaison and observation missions. Its fleet of Criquets was soon supplemented, then replaced by the more modern Cessna L-19 Bird Dog, with the first six being delivered by the Americans in 1956. (ECPA)

The head of the French Air Force flight instructors, Captain Guido, is seen here with one of the Laotian cadets. With the graduation of the first AVRL class, most of the pilots were trained for observation operations. Only a small number were sent to France to be trained as transport pilots. (ECPA)

The Aviation Royale Laotienne (AVRL) was formed on 28 January 1955 with a mixed training-observation squadron with 10 Morane Saulnier MS 500 Criquets, a version of the German Fieseler Fi 156 Storch. The training of the first Laotian military pilots took place at Wattay Airbase (Vientiane) and at an airstrip in Plain of Jars. (ECPA)

The French initially handed over to the AVRL five C-47s, including this one seen in 1955. It still retained its undersurface fuselage and wings painted in black for participation in night dropping missions during the battle of Dien Bien Phu. Six more C-47s were delivered by the Americans in 1956. (Albert Grandolini Collection)

A small transport and communication flight was added to the AVRL with four L-20 Beavers and five C-47s. The Beavers were well appreciated for their ability to land on small airstrips. (Albert Grandolini Collection)

The small Royal Laotian Navy, created in 1952, deployed only patrol boats by its River Squadron, like this French built FOM 8. Some 31 FOM 8, FOM 11, Mytho as well as Privat classes of gunboats were transferred to the Laotians at the end of 1954. (Albert Grandolini Collection)

All roads lead to the Battlefield

The kingdom's fate would be decided on land and communications were the key. There was no railway and, apart from the Mekong, only a few short rivers in the south were navigable, so everything depended upon the road network developed by the French as Routes Coloniales, now renamed Routes National, but they were only partially paved and in many places were simply packed earth.[12] The French had focused upon east-west routes linking Laos with Vietnam, notably Routes 6 and 7 through Sam Neua and Ban Ban, Route 8 from the Napé Pass (also Na Pe or Nha Phao), Route 12 from the Mu Gia Pass and Route 9 through Tchepone. In addition, there was Route 3 from the Mekong to Nam Tha in northwestern Laos. The prime north-south route was Route 13 running from the royal capital of Luang Prabang to Vientiane, then alongside the Mekong into Cambodia, with trail-like Route 4 from North Vietnam ending in Luang Prabang. South of Route 9 there was a road network linking Tchepone, Saravane, Pakse and Attopeu with numerous bridges and fords.

The road networks helped define the four military regions created early in 1955, initially to control only infantry, although from 1956 regional commanders had control of technical and support units within their commands. The indifference of the politicians to military matters, and the remoteness of the general staff in Vientiane, meant the regional commanders were virtually autonomous and could act as warlords.[13] Région Militaire 1 (Military Region) or RM-1, with headquarters in the royal capital of Luang Prabang, consisted of the northern provinces of Phong Saly, Sayabouray, Houa Khong and Luang Prabang. It was under the command of Major Ouane Rattikone (also Rathikoun), briefly a fighter against the French, and as the royal family's favourite he held court in the city. RM-2, commanded by Major Sang Kittirath, a favourite of the MMF/RGL, had its headquarters at Vientiane but controlled the strategically vital north-eastern provinces of Vientiane, Xieng Khouang and Pathet Lao-held Houa Phan.

The two provinces in the upper Panhandle, Khammoane and Savannakhet, formed RM-3 under the command of Major Sing Rattanasamy, who had been one of the first Laotian NCOs in the French Army, a founder member and first Defence Minister of the Lao Issara before rejoining the French Army to become in 1953 its first Laotian battalion commander. The six southern provinces of Attopeu, Champasak, Saravane, Sedone, Sithadone Vapikhamthong formed RM-4 under another of the first Laotian NCOs, the Catholic Major Amkha Soukhavong, a crony or client of the Pakse strong man Prince Boun Oum Na Champassak whose family dominated the region.

The Political Stalemate

From April 1955 the military stalemate was matched by a political stalemate, leaving the country divided. While the French Army had departed Laos and Hanoi withdrawn most of the 4,000 Viet Minh

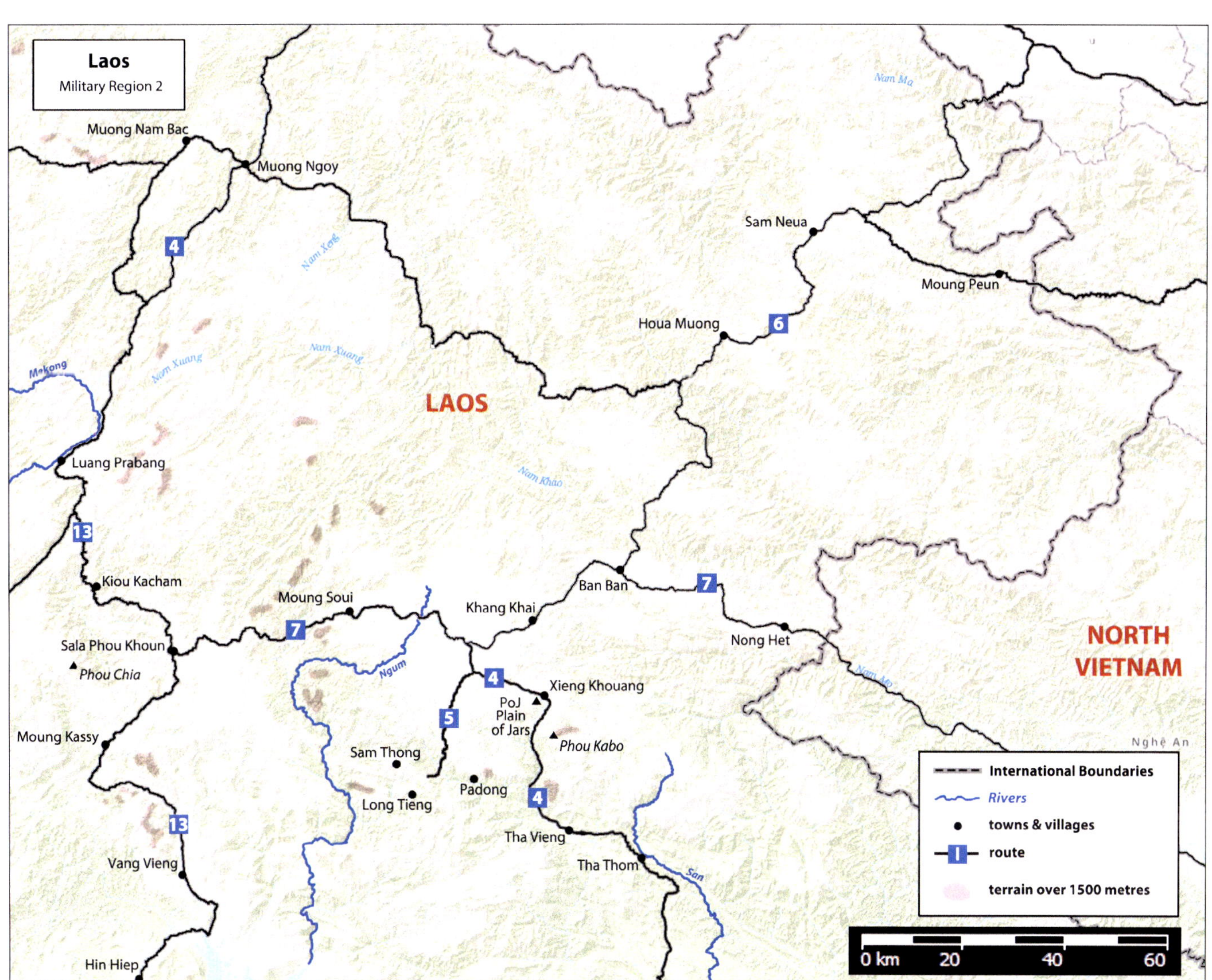

Map of the Military Region 2. (Map by b.b.h.illustrations, based on Ted Hooton)

troops in the country, it decided as early as July 1954 to maintain a formal presence, the Communist Party's General Military Committee and Defence Ministry asking Dao Viet Hung, Deputy Commissar for their forces in Laos, to make proposals. This led to the creation of the Military Advisor Group to aid the Pathet Lao Army, better known as Group 100 because it had 100 cadres. This was under the command of Colonel Chu Huy Man, who was of Tai origin and was the 316th Viet Minh Division's political officer at Dien Bien Phu, and departed Hanoi on 10 August 1954, setting up its headquarters at Ban Na Meo and expanding to 314 military and 650 political advisers, of whom 122 were based in North Vietnam.[14] This supported the expansion of the Pathet Lao 'in all matters' to regional level, and gave the Pathet Lao confidence to deny government officials access to their territory and to maintain a covert military presence on the Bolovens Plateau.

In October 1955 there was a vain bid to break the political stalemate but, unable to make progress, Katay went ahead with national elections on 25 December 1955, although the Pathet Lao refused to allow them in their provinces. When the Premier failed to gain a mandate, he was replaced by a new government under Souvanna Phouma.[15] The Royal Government in Vientiane made a declaration of neutrality in the Cold War, but within it were stridently anti-Communist politicians opposed to the integration of the Pathet Lao and they received covert Thai support. A Right-Wing gang attempted to assassinate Foreign Minister Phoui Sananikone, who was wounded, but Defence Minister Kou Voravong was killed, and the subsequent crisis forced Souvanna Phouma to resign and be replaced by Katay Don Sasorit's government. The new premier opened negotiations with Souphanouvong over the political future of the country, but the divisions within each side were aggravated by personal antagonism because the chief negotiators were both former Lao Issara members.

Souvanna Phuma optimistically believed that, left alone, the Lao could settle their differences and that he could persuade his younger half-brother Souphanouvong to join a neutralist coalition government and thwart external intervention. A moderate, stoical Francophile who had married a French woman, he failed to recognise the commitment of his energetic, headstrong, ambitious and assertive half-brother, willing to work with the Vietnamese to organise a social/political revolution and to create a nation which would fit into the Communist bloc.[16] Yet Vientiane continued to steer the country in the neutralist direction, joining the Non-Aligned Bloc of nations established at Bandung in April 1955 to demonstrate the country posed no threat to its Communist neighbours China and North Vietnam.

A month earlier, on 25 March, the Pathet Lao established Lao People's Revolutionary Party, with Kaysone Phomvihane as Secretary General and Defence Minister, dissolving the Free Lao Front and replacing it with the Lao Patriotic Front (Naeo Lao Hak Sat), or LPF, as an umbrella anti-government movement, similar to the South Vietnamese National Liberation Front, its first congress in January 1956 appointing Souphanouvong as President.[17] The Pathet Lao recognised that the Lao People's Party was still struggling, by December 1956 it had only 2,289 members organised in some 334 cells.[18] Souphanouvong, known as the Red Prince, was born to a commoner and was well-educated and multilingual in eight languages including Greek and Latin. He had married a Vietnamese woman and until 1945 was a civil engineer. The half Lao, half Vietnamese Kaysone was the movement's real leader but deliberately remained in the background because of his pro-Vietnamese views, lowly origins and lack of charisma. He emerged from the shadows only when the Pathet Lao took power in 1975 replacing figurehead Souphanouvong who was articulate and had charisma.[19] In fact, the Vietnamese Communists, or Lao Dong, secretly ran the Pathet Lao through the Party Affairs Committee under Nguyen Khang.[20]

With Laos firmly in the neutral camp, the Pathet Lao, who were renamed the Neo Lao Issara (Free Laos Front) the Lao Patriotic Front in 1956, now faced growing pressure from its sponsors to compromise. When Souvanna and Souphanouvong met in Vientiane in August 1956, the Pathet Lao reluctantly agreed to integrate their two provinces and forces within a government of national union. There were also to be a new round of national elections, and in December 1956 it was agreed they would be held once the LPF was recognised as a political party. Electoral preparations were completed in February 1957 but within the National Assembly there were calls for the integration of the Pathet Lao to precede, rather than follow, the establishment of the new government. This opposition forced Souvanna's resignation on 30 May 1957, leading to a two-month-long political crisis that saw Souvanna's opponents unable to form a government. He returned to steer the agreement through the Assembly and on 18 November it was formally accepted by Souphanouvong, followed, the next day, by the approval of the new government. There was still opposition from the other elite families because, essentially, the agreement was virtually a family matter for the two half-brothers.

The Pathet Lao military organisation was bolstered by the clandestine PAVN Advisory Group 100, seen here in Sam Nuea in 1956. Its commander, Chu Huy Man is third from left, standing. (PAVN)

After months of negotiations, an agreement was finally signed between Souvanna Phouma, on the right, and Souphanouvong, on his left, on 19 November 1957, for the constitution of a coalition cabinet as stipulated by the Geneva Accords. (Albert Grandolini Collection)

The 1958 Election

Implementation of the August 1956 agreement did not begin until January 1958, when Vientiane sent troops to impose its authority in Houa Phan and Phong Saly. A joint administration was established in Houa Phan under the ANL's Major Khong Vongnarath in Sam Neua, and Sakoun's guerrillas became an augmented infantry battalion (Batailon Volontaires 23 – BV 23), while BI 7, redesignated BI 22, moved into Sam Neua.[21] For their part, the Pathet Lao began preparing for demobilisation from late 1957 and handed the International Control Commission (ICC) 2,915 rifles, 1,311 submachine guns, 275 light and 23 medium machine guns, 65 mortars, and a dozen 75mm recoilless rifles. The ICC delegates from Canada (West), Poland (East) and India (Neutral) were to monitor cease-fire violations and make objective observations which would help restore peace. However, they were handicapped by a lack of transport and the fact the Pathet Lao usually denied it access to their territories, these problems were exacerbated by differences between the members. Consequently, the ICC was unable to provide even nominal monitoring within Pathet Lao-controlled territory, so they were unaware that Kaysone was transferring troops into North Vietnam to act as both operational reserve and an insurance policy.

Meanwhile, Pathet Lao officials entered the government, with Souphanouvong one of two Pathet Lao ministers responsible for Planning and Reconstruction, and preparations began to merge the two armies. The elections for 21 National Assembly seats were vigorously contested, the Pathet Lao and their LPF allies the Party of Peace Through Neutrality (Santhiphap Pen Kang), established in July 1956 by the pro-Communist half-Chinese Quinim Pholsena, fielding 13 candidates including Kaysone Phomvihane, who contested Attopeu province. The Pathet Lao were more astute than their rivals, focusing upon key provinces and the discontented minorities within them, giving and receiving a free hand from their LPF allies while their Right/Centre opponents would field several candidates in each province diluting the pro-government vote. Unlike the Left, they made no attempt at creating a political organisation at village level, while the Pathet Lao despatched cadres who won support with educational and health work as well as spreading the revolutionary message. Curiously, it was only in Attopeu that the Pathet Lao used intimidation and coercion but when the count was completed in May, it was generally accepted the elections had been free and fair.

The result was a shock for the Right, with the Pathet Lao winning nine seats (43% of the total) and Souphanouvong being the top national vote-winner to become chairman of the National Assembly. The situation was aggravated by the fact that the Pathet Lao's allies, the Santiphab Party won four seats, giving the Left 62% of the vote. The Right quickly formed an anti-Communist Rally of the Lao People (Lao Huam Lao) as an umbrella organisation for clan interests under Katay, Souvanna Phouma and the conservative leader Phoui Sananikone (Phuy Xananikon). The Left's triumph was short-lived, for they needed members of the Right and Centre to form the required coalition government in which Souvanna Phouma was still the Premier. But, neither side had sufficient power to form the coalition government with each depending upon votes from independents or the Voravong clan's Democratic Party.

The conservatives reacted vigorously to their election defeat, with leading young conservative military, diplomatic and senior administrators creating in mid-June the Committee for the Defence of the National Interest (Comité pour la Défense des Interêts Nationaux), or CDNI, which, within a month, engineered a vote of confidence forcing out Souvanna Phouma and his government. The CDNI helped to organise under the conservative Nationalist Party's Phoui Sananikone a new government, which included four CDNI members whom Phoui did not trust.

After losing the election at the National Assembly, the Right succeeded in derailing the first coalition government with the Pathet Lao by creating a new government on 18 August 1958. Heading it was Premier Phoui Sananikone, here at the right, receiving United Nations General Secretary Dag Hammarskjold, who went to Vientiane on 9 March 1959 to enquire about the incursions of North Vietnamese forces. (United Nations)

Western Reaction

The United States reacted to growing Communist power and influence in Asia by emulating the Truman Doctrine which had been so successful in post-war Europe. The doctrine under President Harry Truman aimed to create anti-communist bilateral and collective defence treaties to contain Communist power, and had been successful in Europe where it led to the North Atlantic Treaty Organisation (NATO). The philosophy was inherited by his successor, President Dwight D. Eisenhower, who issued National Security Council resolution 5429/2 on 20 August 1954. This sought to meet Communist insurgency in South-East Asia within the Geneva Accords, with Thailand now regarded as the keystone to US regional strategy. Just as Great Britain and France had been the foundation of NATO, the Thais would be one of the founders of a new organisation for military security in Asia, SEATO.

The 700-year-old Thai kingdom had survived colonial expansion by the Europeans in the 19th century and the Japanese in the 1940s through skilful diplomacy, which continued into the Cold War. Bangkok decided to develop a close relationship with Washington after recognising the United States was now the leading power in what is now called the Pacific Rim, and this was implemented when the stridently anti-communist Field Marshal Plaek Phibunsongkhram returned to power in November 1947. For their part the Americans were seeking Asian friends and began providing Thailand military aid from 1949, and when Phibunsongkhram aligned his country with the United States during the Korean War, Washington made his country the heart of US Far Eastern policy and the primary recipient of aid in the region. However, Thailand was ambivalent about relations with Laos, and during the latter stages of the French Indochina War its Border Patrol Police (BPP) made little attempt to stop cross-border raids by surviving Lao Issara forces.[22]

Washington was also concerned about the temporarily divided Vietnam, which was to be unified following a referendum. The West did not anticipate fair elections in North Vietnam where the Communists brutally suppressed their political opponents and were strong politically in South Vietnam, where their opponents were ill-organised and fragmented, bringing the prospect of a Communist united Vietnam. But, South Vietnam's Premier, Ngo Dinh Diem, refused in July 1955 to accept the terms of the Geneva Accords arguing that, although South Vietnam was part of the French Union, it was not a signatory of the agreement and, he also claimed, correctly, there could be no fair elections in the north. He used his limited military forces to crush his rivals, and by October 1955 was strong enough to hold his own referendum which supported an independent Republic of South Vietnam, of which he became

An M3 half-track of the armoured squadron of the RM-5 placed under Phoumi Nosavan's forces during the battle of Vientiane in December 1960. Nominally, the armoured and reconnaissance squadrons were part of the ANL Armoured Regiment but were dispersed within the various military regions. This vehicle was armed with no less than three French-built MAC-31A2 7.65mm machine guns. (Artwork by David Bocquelet)

An M5 Stuart light tank of the Tank Squadron of the ANL Armoured Regiment during the fighting against the Pathet Lao and North Vietnamese around Sam Nuea in 1959. Laos received some fifteen M5s that were later replaced by M24 Chaffees. (Artwork by David Bocquelet)

An ANL M8 Greyhound of Groupement Mobile B (GM B) that operated along Route 13 during the Phoumi Nosavan advance from Savannakhet to retake Vientiane in December 1960. (Artwork by David Bocquelet)

Another ANL M8 of the Reconnaissance Squadron of the ANL Armoured Regiment during the battle of Vientiane in December 1960. Laos received 13 M8 Greyhounds along with 19 M3 scout cars and 20 M3 half-tracks. (Artwork by David Bocquelet)

An M24 Chaffee of the Tank Squadron of the ANL Armoured Regiment during the battle of Vientiane in December 1960. Laos received 15 M24s, these replaced the M5 Stuart light tanks. (Artwork by David Bocquelet)

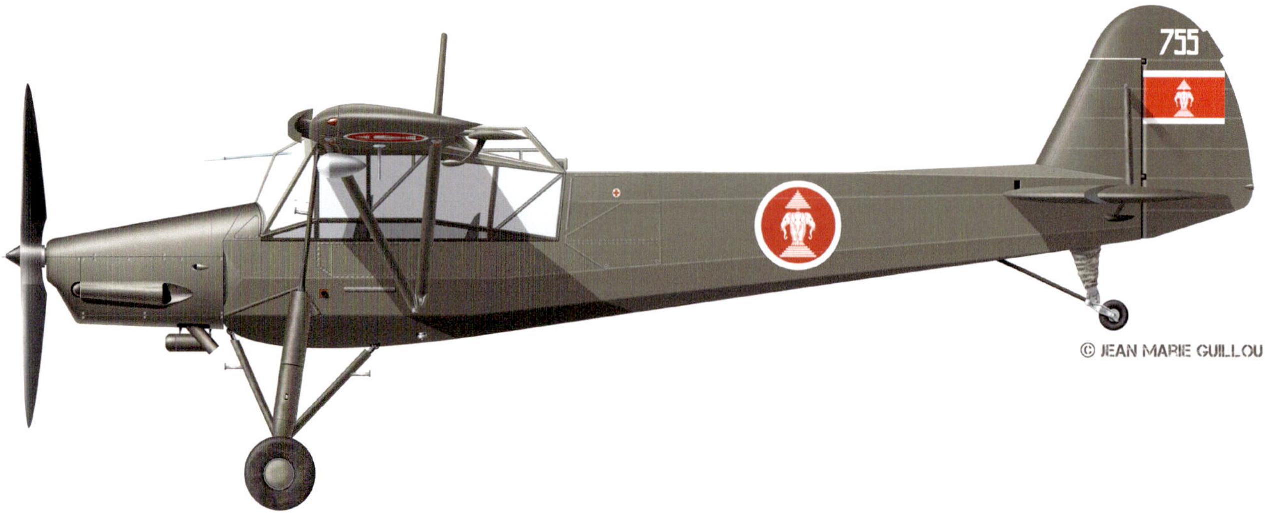

An AVRL Morane Saulnier MS 500 Criquet, the French version of the German Fieseler F 156 Storch that equipped most of the French and Vietnamese air observations squadrons during the Indochina War. Laos inherited ten from 1955 that served both for training, liaison, and observation tasks. (Artwork by Jean-Marie Guillou)

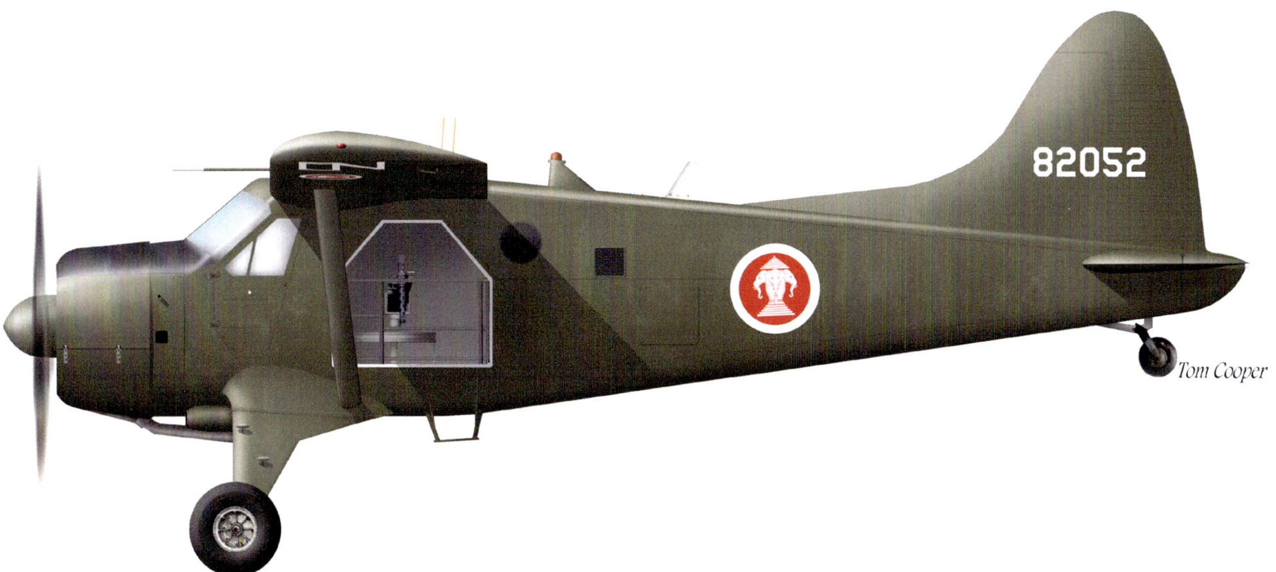

The RLAF initially received four DHC L-20 Beavers in 1956 from the United States and they served in a mixed liaison/transport squadron with C-47s. During the fighting opposing ANL to the Neutralists of Kong Le in 1961, at least one Beaver was armed with a 7.62mm machine gun on the left side door to serve as a gunship. (Artwork by Tom Cooper)

An RLAF C-47 seen at Wattay Airbase (Vientiane) in 1955. It was one of the original five C-47s delivered by the French and still retained its undersurface fuselage and wings painted in black for night parachuting missions during the Dien Bien Phu battle of the previous year. At that date, the Laotian C-47s were crewed by French instructors due to the lack of qualified Laotian personnel. (Artwork by Jean-Marie Guillou)

France maintained a mixed air group at Seno Airbase until 1963, when the base was relinquished to the Laotians. It included six DHC L-20s. They were particularly appreciated for their STOL capabilities. Some were involved in clandestine operations of the French SDCE Intelligence alongside civilian Beavers and Max-Holste MH-1521 Broussards of the Veha Akat air taxi company. (Artwork by Tom Cooper)

The French mixed air group of Seno also included a half-dozen C-47s. This particular aircraft was regularly detached to Hanoi, between August 1956 and May 1957, in support of the French Foreign Affairs Ministry's representative, Jean Sainteny. It also helped to exfiltrate a defecting Czechoslovakian diplomat from North Vietnam. (Artwork by Jean-Marie Guillou)

The French Seno Airbase also hosted some Sikorsky H-19 helicopters detached from the Armée de l'Air 65th Helicopter Wing stationed at Tan Son Nhut Airbase, South Vietnam, until 1958. They were mainly used to support the various French instructional teams in Laos as well as for the displacements of the observers of the International Control Commission. (Artwork by Tom Cooper)

Thailand's involvement in Laos started as soon as 1955 by dispatching two RTAF Sikorsky H-19s without military markings, and which were officially Air Laos helicopters, to support the ANL. When fighting resumed with Pathet Lao in 1959, at least four H-19s of the RTAF 63rd Squadron of the 6th Wing at Don Muang Airbase (Bangkok) were forwarded to airfields of northern Thailand to fly missions across the Mekong River. (Artwork by Tom Cooper)

By 1950 the United States had brought in massive amounts of military equipment to modernise and expand the Thai armed forces. Thailand would be at the forefront of the Cold War and would shield Malaya and Singapore in case of communist take-over of French Indochina. The RTAF was one of the main beneficiaries by receiving no less than 204 Grumman F8F1 Bearcats between 1951 and 1955. They equipped ten squadrons of the 1st, 2nd, 4th and 5th Wings. This F8F1 of the 12th Squadron of the 1st Wing was based at Don Muang Airbase in 1956. (Artwork by Jean-Marie Guillou)

The creation of the Southeast Asia Treaty Organisation (SEATO), with its seat at Bangkok, on 8 September 1954, saw Thailand as the first Southeast Asian country introducing fighter jets into service when 31 F-84G Thunderjets were delivered in 1956. This F-84G was operated by the 12th Squadron of the 1st Wing at Don Muang Airbase in 1958. (Artwork by Tom Cooper)

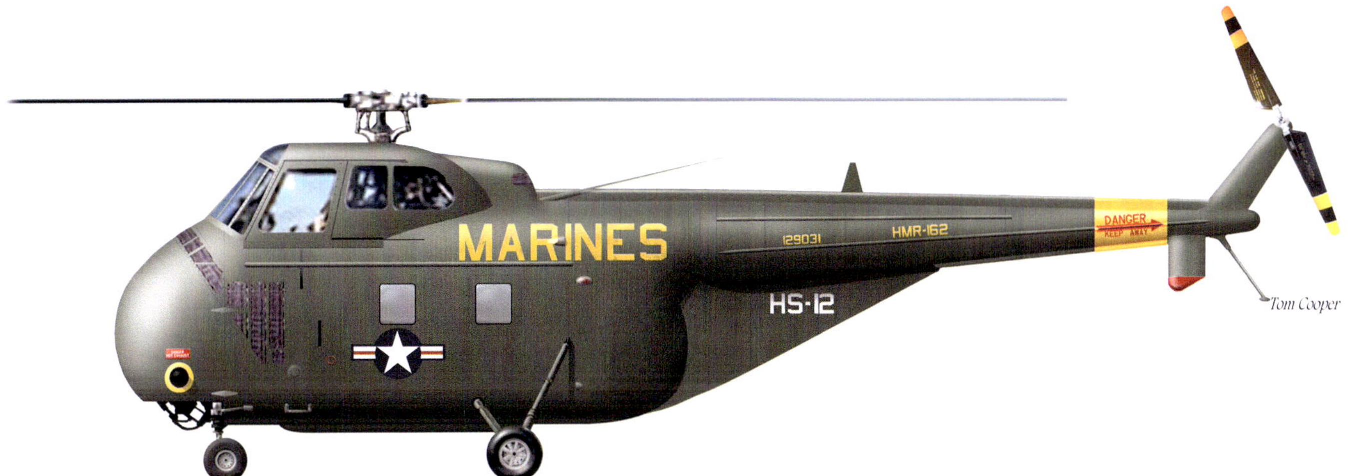

The first significant SEATO exercise, Operation Firm Link, took place in Thailand in February 1956, involving British, New Zealand, Philippines, Thai, and United States troops. The troops were engaged in air assault operations with USMC helicopters of the HMR-161, HMR-162 and HMR-163 Squadrons, operating out the anti-submarine carrier USS *Princeton* (CVS-37). This HRS-3 of the HMR-162 Squadron, the Marine version of the H-19B, was used to ferry Philippine and US Marine troops in the area of Bangkok. (Artwork by Tom Cooper)

A USAF F-84G of the 9th Fighter Bomber Squadron of the 49th Fighter Bomber Wing. Deployed to Thailand for Operation Firm Link in February 1956 from Misawa Airbase, Japan, with the last leg, from Philippines to Dong Muang Airbase, Thailand, with the help of KB-29 tankers, demonstrating the USAF's newly acquired air-to-air refuelling capability. The aircraft is shown here armed with a pair of AN-M58 500lb bombs. (Artwork by Jean-Marie Guillou)

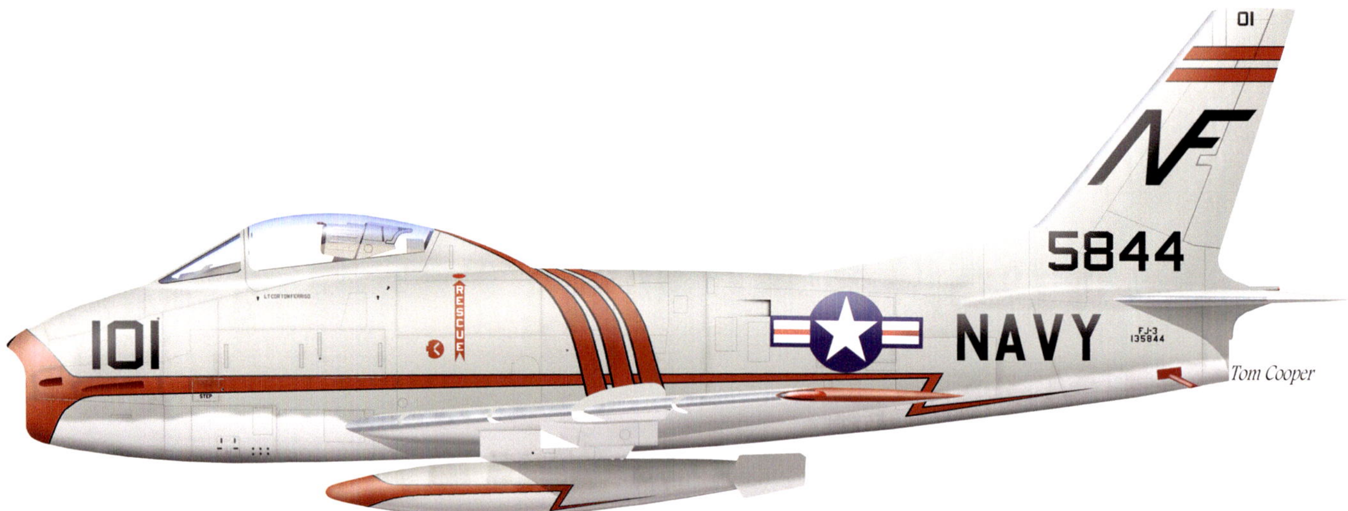

A US Navy North American FJ-3 Fury of the VF-51 Squadron of the Carrier Air Group 5 (CVG-5) operating on the carrier USS *Bon Homme Richard* (CVA-31) in December 1957. While the US Navy 7th Fleet was mobilised until that date for possible crisis in Korea or Taiwan, it now extended its exercises into the South China Sea in relation to the unravelling situation in Vietnam and Laos. (Artwork by Tom Cooper)

A US Navy Douglas F4D-1 Skyray of the VF-141 Squadron of the Group 5 (CVG-5) operating on the carrier USS *Bon Homme Richard* (CVA-31) in December 1957. The carrier was part of the intervention force, the Task Force 77, of the US Navy 7th Fleet with contingency plans to support SEATO. Note the AAM-N-7 (a.k.a. GAR-8) – subsequently AIM-9B Sidewinder – air-to-air missile on the outboard underwing pylon. The US Navy was one of the first in the world to deploy operationally air-to-air missiles on its interceptors. (Artwork by Tom Cooper)

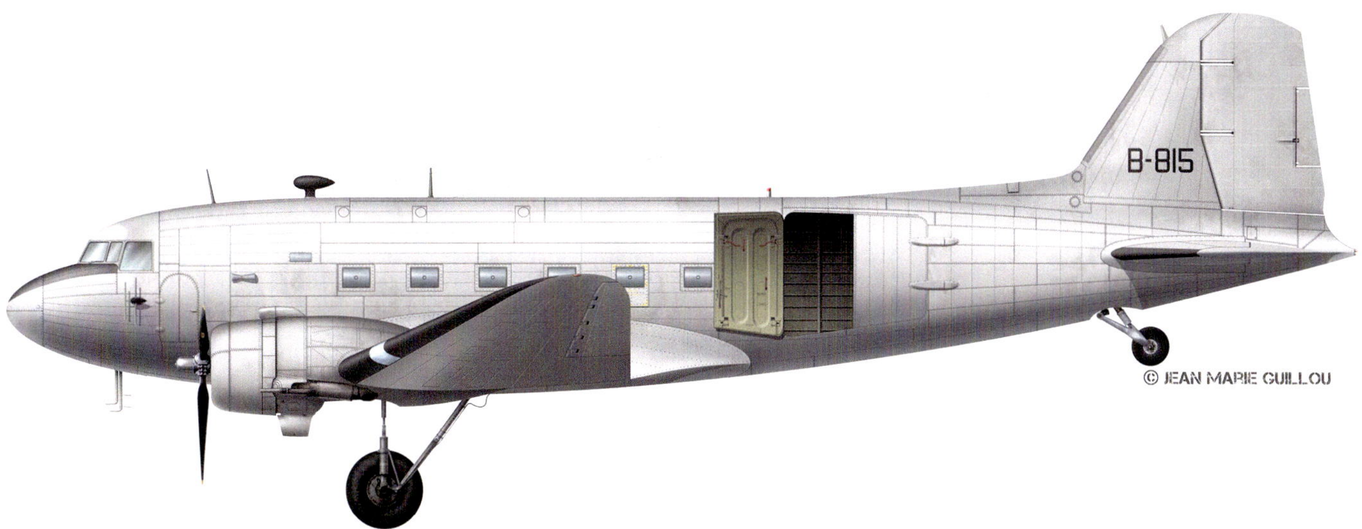

An Air America C-47A seen operating in Laos in 1959 in support of the introduction of US Special Forces (Operation Hotfoot). As with most of the aircraft operated by the CIA's 'airline', it adopted a very inconspicuous livery with its only marking being its Taiwanese registered serial number. The aircraft here illustrated later crashed while operating in support of the Royal Thai Border Police in Songkhla, Thailand, on 27 December 1963, killing the twelve people onboard. (Artwork by Jean-Marie Guillou)

In a departure from the cautious Soviet policy towards the conflict in Southeast Asia, in December 1960 Moscow decided to intervene directly in Laos in support of the Neutralist troops of Kong Le and their Pathet Lao allies by organising an airbridge between North Vietnam and the areas held by the rebels in Laos. One of the first Soviet Air Force transport units involved was the 194th Transport Regiment of Ivanovo, which operated Il-14s. In order to disguise their true identity, the aircraft received false Aeroflot airline markings, and the crew wore civilian clothes. (Artwork by Tom Cooper)

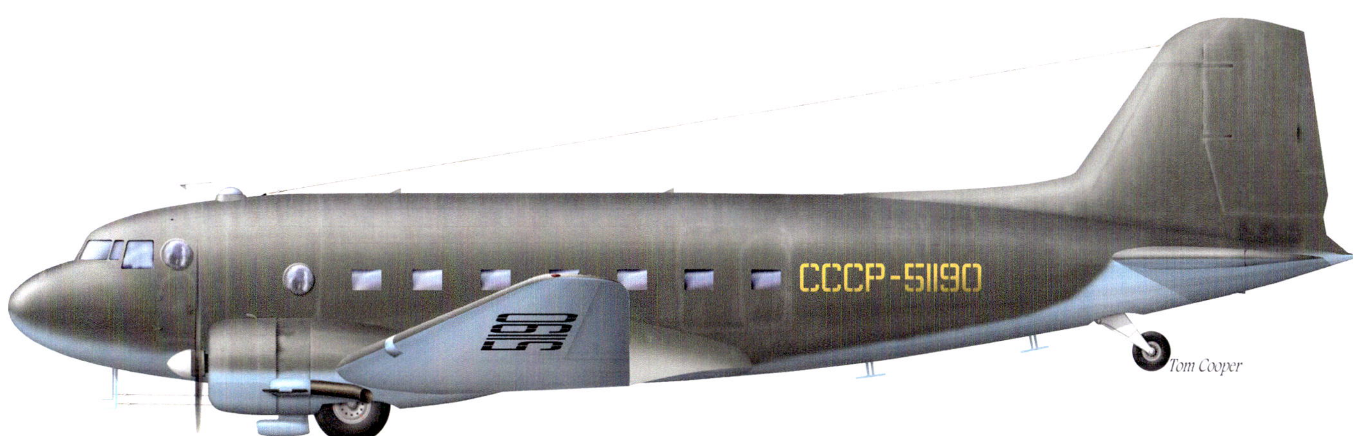

As the transportation needs increased for the support of the Neutralist forces in the Plain of Jars, Moscow rushed in additional aircraft from the Soviet Air Force's Military Transport Aviation (Voyenno – Transportnoy Aviatsii – VTA), including Lisunov Li-2s of the 338th Transport Regiment. While for most of their planes the Soviets made efforts to disguise them in 'Aeroflot' airliners, the urgency of the situation left many airframes in their original military camouflage scheme with the addition of a 'civilian' registration number. This aircraft of the 4th Squadron of the regiment was piloted by Captain D. B. Dubovcev, who operated from Gia Lam Airbase (Hanoi) in 1961 and 1962. (Artwork by Tom Cooper)

(Map by Anderson Subtil, based on Ted Hooton's references)

president. By January 1957 the ICC reluctantly recognised that neither part of Vietnam had honoured the Geneva Accords.

The United States was quick to support Diem as an anti-Communist strong man, and began nearly two decades of huge financial investment, but if they had hoped to control him they quickly discovered the tail was wagging the dog. Diem's government was essentially a dictatorship with rigid control exacerbated by extensive corruption. As he was supported by large landowners, he gave only half-hearted support to what would have been vote-winning land reform, and rather than seeking political support he demanded obedience from the population. His security forces sought to destroy the remnants of the Viet Minh organisation in the south, stimulating their resistance in defiance to instructions from Hanoi. This resistance found fertile support among the peasantry becoming the Viet Cong, an acronym for Vietnamese Communist (Viet Nam cong san), who would quickly create the National Liberation Army (Quan Doi Giai Phong) or Liberation Army of South Vietnam (Quan Giai phong mien Nam Viet Nam), although the term VC will be used for both the movement and its forces in this series.

Within Laos the first full US ambassador from 1 November 1954 was Charles W. Yost, a career diplomat who would remain in position until 27 April 1956. By the time he arrived, an American aid programme was well under way, totalling $120 million from 1955 to 1958, in a mixture of cash grants and commodity imports to soak up some of this money and control inflation. The aid was largely aimed at providing indirect support for military operations, indeed 84 per cent ($30 million) of the annual cash grant was for army pay and local procurement, while most of the $184 million spent on communications up to 1959 was for projects which supported military operations, with only $1.3 million on agriculture. With little oversight, American economic aid encouraged corruption on a massive scale within Laos but provided strong American influence on the political process. Congressional criticism of the Laotian government's handling of American aid led to its suspension on 30 June 1958, the end of the financial year.[23]

In February and March 1955, the US State Secretary John Foster Dulles toured Asiatic capitals to promote the newly created South East Asia Treaty Organisation (SEATO). He went to Vientiane on 27 February to reaffirm to the Laotians American support and to try to convince them to steer away from any coalition government with the Communists, as stipulated by the Geneva Accords. (Albert Grandolini Collection)

The results of the Laotian elections of May 1958, which left the Pathet Lao and its allies firmly within the coalition government, caused the Americans great concern. It reminded them of Czechoslovakia, where Communists joining the democratically-elected government had steadily tightened their grip on the police, the army and intelligence organisations as well as establishing a militia. In 1948 the militia staged a coup d'état and the Communists took control of the state, purging their opponents and quickly establishing a regime similar to the Soviet Union. In contingency planning, the US Defense Department believed the prime threat in Asia was from China and in particular feared some form of conventional attack similar to the one which had opened the Korean War. The planning in the early 1950s had given Northeast Asia priority in operations, although the Pentagon anticipated that an advance through Indochina and Thailand would be vigorously defended only along the Kra Peninsula, essentially to protect the British bases in Singapore.[24] However, President Eisenhower favoured a forward defence to contain China, and if this was successful it might be followed by a counter-offensive which might possibly include those Chinese Nationalist troops who had been driven out of their homeland and taken refuge in Burma. On the basis of experience during French operations against the Viet Minh, Washington did not believe the Laotians would pose a significant threat to a Chinese advance, but believed Thailand would be a better bet and for this reason the Americans concentrated on strengthening Thailand through SEATO, with the first major exercise in February 1956.

As well as overt military aid for Laos, Washington also organised covert military support through the CIA and Thai forces. The CIA was interested in irregular forces, supplying 8,000 weapons to the AD troops, but also operated CAT which provided air support while Bangkok, at the urging of the US Embassy, became involved in training. The Royal Thai Army (RTA) began this in March 1955, and the Royal Thai Air Force provided two H-19 helicopters operating from Wattay Airbase to support ANL operations. The BPP also controlled the training and expansion of the Laotian Police, which grew from 500 to 4,000 men, with over 100 vehicles. Most recruits were trained in Thailand, with an emphasis on political control to fight insurgency making the Laotian Police a paramilitary organisation.[25] However, Bangkok believed that co-operation should be through SEATO, while the potential involvement of the Pathet Lao in the Laotian government increased Thai concerns about the future of the country and, for this reason, co-operation was put on hold during 1956.[26]

But, the Americans were not the only foreigners involved in Laotian affairs. Hanoi officially aimed to improve relations with the new Laotian and Cambodian governments while covertly assisting

Thailand became one of the main recipients of the SEATO aid programme to modernise and expand its armed forces. Some $686 million of military aid was furnished between 1950 and 1965. Bangkok would receive new equipment for the 85,000 strong Royal Thai Army (RTA), including 86 M24 Chaffee tanks, which replaced the 40 obsolete Second World War Japanese Type 95 HA-GO light tanks. (Albert Grandolini Collection)

The RTA also received 68 M2A1 105mm guns which replaced the 150 Japanese Type 38 75mm field guns. (Albert Grandolini Collection)

The Royal Thai Air Force (RTAF) also greatly benefitted from Thailand adhesion to SEATO. From 1954 to 1960, the service received some 368 aircraft from United States, including 31 F-84G Thunderjets and 40 F-86F Saber jets. The first fighters delivered were 129 Gruman F8F1 Bearcat. (Albert Grandolini Collection)

American instructors of the Joint United States Military Advisory Group Thailand (JUSMAGTHAI) overseeing a review of one of the new RTA units re-equipped with US military equipment in 1958. (Albert Grandolini Collection)

During this review the Americans presented M16 multiple gun motor carriages. Based on an M3 half-track chassis, they had a M45 mounting of quad 0.50 calibre (12.7mm) M2 machine guns for anti-aircraft and direct infantry support roles. (Albert Grandolini Collection)

their national communist parties.[27] Yet Hanoi had a low opinion of the Pathet Lao leadership and felt the country was a shambles which they could not repair, and as early as 15 October 1954, the Politburo made it clear it was ignoring the conditions of non-interference in Laotian internal affairs. It stated: 'No matter how the situation develops, we must use all efforts to strengthen the task of consolidating the two provinces, building the army, building the people's foundation and push forward the political struggle … all over the country ….'[28] On 10 April 1955, the VWP created the Lao and Cambodian Central Committee, under Le Duc Tho, to monitor events, advise the VWP Central Committee and train cadres to operate in those countries.[29]

It continued to influence events through Group 100, now commanded by Col Dinh Van Tuy, and by the end of 1957 had expanded to 849 members, although many advisors were on rotation.[30] The advisors trained and equipped the Pathet Lao, who had attracted 10,000-15,000 young people to their territory, but the emphasis was upon political activity and two political schools (T50 and T51) were created in North Vietnam for cadre training on 22 June 1957. Pathet Lao military strength was restricted, and by early 1957 had 7,518 men with nine main battalions, 11 independent companies, and three engineer, transport, and security companies. The North Vietnamese also provided their Laotian friends with financial support and 'Laos thus became the only country in the world at the time where the armed forces on both sides of a civil conflict were entirely financed by foreign powers'.[31]

Direct military intervention remained an option for Hanoi which, at the beginning of 1955, earmarked the 335th Division in North Vietnam's Moc Chau Highlands for possible operations in Laos. The division was dissolved in November 1957, then reformed as a brigade ready to help consolidate the Pathet Lao control of Houa Phan and Phong Saly. In 1958, the former 316th PAVN Division was also downsized to a brigade with its three regiments, as well as its artillery regiment, deployed close to the border of northern and central Laos to protect the engineering units working on the expanded logistic corridor that was steadily advancing south.[32] Hanoi's growing confidence in the likelihood of a friendly government in Laos led to the decision to disband Group 100 in January 1958, after a surge in both training and political indoctrination, with training continuing after its departure. Simultaneously, PAVN forces along the border were reduced, the 335th Brigade becoming a regiment with responsibility for potential cross-border operations divided between Brigadier Bang Giang's Northwest Military Region (headquarters Son La), with responsibility for northern Laos, and the 4th Military Region (headquarters Vinh) covering central and southern Laos. The remainder of brigade was committed to economic and engineering work.[33]

Ho Chi Minh came in person to assess the availability of the 335th Brigade to return to Laos. He is being shown the weapons of the brigade's artillery battalion, including (from left to right) an 81mm mortar, a Japanese Type 92 70mm light howitzer, an M2A1 105mm gun, and an M1 75mm pack howitzer. (PAVN)

When the Pathet Lao joined a coalition government in Vientiane, the PAVN reduced the 335th Division to a brigade at the end of 1957, but its operational status increased when the government came under pressure from the Right-wing CDNI. Ho Chi Minh is seen here inspecting the brigade at Moc Chau in early 1959. (PAVN)

SEATO

The idea of an Asian NATO came from several American sources, including Vice President Richard P. Nixon, and won the support of Secretary of State John Foster Dulles, Southeast Asia the focus of attention.

Anti-Communist nations held a conference in Manila, which led on 8 September 1954 to the Southeast Asia Collective Defence Treaty or Manila Pact, although only three Asian nations; Pakistan, the Philippines and Thailand, were signatories together with the United States, the United Kingdom, France, Australia, and New Zealand, who would provide 75 per cent of the funding. The Southeast Asia Treaty Organisation (SEATO) was formally established on 15 February 1955, in Bangkok where a US Military Assistance and Advisory Group (MAAG) was created to channel Washington's military aid, including $92 million for facilities between 1954 and 1962. From its earliest days SEATO offered Laos and Cambodia protection from external Communist aggression in a protocol which excluded South Vietnam, because it did not recognise the Geneva Accords. This provided the justification for US overt and covert military intervention in Indochina, especially in Vietnam where it was supported by Australia and New Zealand. At SEATO's inaugural meeting the new alliance offered Laos protection from any external Communist threat, but neither France nor Great Britain would support overt military action unless there was direct Chinese intervention, and they frowned at covert action.[34]

The scenario of SEATO's first major exercise, Operation Firm Link, in February 1956, tested the ability to respond to the threat of an invasion of Thailand through Laos. US Army, a battalion of the 3rd Marines as well as Filipinos came to 'support' the Royal Thai Army (RTA). The Marines were flown in by HMR-161, HMR-162 and HMR-163 from the anti-submarine carrier USS *Princeton*, which later became an amphibious assault carrier, while the cruisers and destroyers of the US 7th Fleet task group were reinforced by a cruiser as well as five destroyers and frigates from the Royal Navy, the Royal Australian and Royal New Zealand navies. The Royal Thai Air Force (RTAF) F-84G Thunderjets, F8F-1/2 Bearcats and Dakotas were reinforced by USAF Thunderjets of the 49th Fighter-Bomber Wing as well as C-119 and C-124 transports, Venoms of both 60 Squadron RAF and 14 Squadron RNZAF, which also supplied Bristol Freighters. A battery of M50 Honest John surface-to-surface rockets was also deployed to simulate tactical nuclear strikes.

This exercise set a precedent for subsequent shows of force until 1964, which were usually related to crises in Laos. But SEATO's European contributors, the United Kingdom and France, were finding it increasingly difficult to maintain world-wide commitments and were forced to focus their efforts on supporting major counter-insurgency missions, with the British deploying more than 30,000 troops in Malaya against largely Chinese Communist guerrillas, as well as troops in Cyprus and Kenya against nationalists, while France would eventually deploy more than 500,000 in Algeria against a nationalist movement. These commitments meant the French were unable to provide more than a token force for SEATO, while the British contribution was limited forcing the Americans to realise that in the event of a Chinese invasion, they would have to shoulder most of the burden.

The first SEATO exercise, Operation Firm Link, took place in Thailand in February 1956 to test rapid deployment capability of multinational forces. For two weeks, it involved US, Thai, British, New Zealand, and Philippines forces. These HRS-3 (The Marine version of the Sikorsky S-19) helicopters of the US Marines Squadron HMR-162 are seen during an air assault exercise near Bangkok. (USMC)

This USMC HRS-3 helicopter is seen during another air assault exercise with Philippine troops. (USMC)

USAF C-119s at Dong Muang Airbase, Bangkok, during Operation Firm Link. They were used for several parachute dropping exercises with RTAF C-47s. (USAF)

In addition to the RAF and RNZAF Venom FB.4s, Operation Firm Link also saw the participation of the F-84Gs Thunderjets of the USAF 49th Fighter-Bomber Wing. The aircraft had flown in from their home base of Misawa, Japan, after several air-to-air refuelling operations with KB-29 tankers. Note the refuelling boom on the left-wing external fuel tip tank on the aircraft on the foreground. (USAF)

A battery of M50 Honest John unguided surface-to-surface rockets was also deployed to simulate tactical nuclear strikes during Operation Firm Link. The rocket system is displayed here during a military parade at Bangkok at the conclusion of the exercise. (US Army)

4

THE RIGHT STRIKES BACK

In January 1959 three CDNI members, including Defence Minister Colonel Phoumi Novasan, replaced Souvanna Phouma's allies in the cabinet and these reduced Premier Phoui to a figurehead. The CDNI, with American encouragement, also demanded that the ICC, the international guarantor of the country's military neutrality, quit the country leading to Indian and Polish protests. Reluctantly, the ICC ended its activities in July, but remained in Laos until the following February. The Right-Wing government quickly displayed pro-American views and recognised the governments of Taiwan's Republic of China and South Vietnam, the former opening a consulate and the latter a full embassy to compete with Hanoi's.[1]

Phoumi was a soft-spoken man from Savannakhet with an open smile and persuasive manner, but always there was a hint of restrained violence, and someone who knew him well observed: 'He was hated and feared, and his orders were obeyed'.[2] Interestingly, Phoumi was a first cousin of Thailand's Field Marshal Thanarat Sarit who would overthrow Plaek in September 1957.[3] Phoumi and the CDNI began raising public concern about the North Vietnamese threat, beginning with an incident on 15 December 1958, when a ANL patrol operating within disputed territory in a remote mountain valley opposite the Vietnamese Demilitarised Zone (DMZ) were fired on. The perpetrators were never identified but were probably North Vietnamese soldiers, for Hanoi was using the area to send cadres into South Vietnam. Premier Phoui used this incident, and reports of PAVN troops massing on the border, to pass a law allowing him to rule for a year without interference from the Assembly, but increasingly, it was the FAL under Phoumi which became the arbiter of policy.

Arrests and Assassinations

The government now arrested Pathet Lao activists and assassinated some others, especially in Phong Saly, with many cadres fleeing across the border. In May the planned integration of Pathet Lao forces failed and some abandoned their camps and headed into the jungle, but the Communists still retained a presence in Vientiane, operating with the legitimacy of the Vientiane Agreements. Then, on 25 May, the CDNI decided to arrest the Pathet Lao leaders in Vientiane, but dithered and it was not until 28 July that security forces seized 16, including Souphanouvong. Phoui belatedly recognised the harm this was causing, especially in rural areas, but his attempts to put the armed forces/CDNI genie back into the bottle failed. For its part, the Pathet Lao decided to re-embark upon armed struggle, although recognising it faced an uphill battle against a force of 29,000 when its own strength was about 7,000. Meanwhile, Hanoi's reaction was surprisingly muted, being confined merely to protests, but that was because something far more significant was in the wind.[4]

National stability was further undermined by the death, on 29 October, of the popular and respected King Sisavong Vong, who had ruled for 55 years. He was succeeded by Crown Prince Savang Vatthana, a physically imposing man with only a tenuous grasp of politics who had always lived in his father's shadow, and would now be little more than a figurehead. 'Though well-travelled and honest, the prince was thought to lack the respect and enthusiasm needed to control the warring factions pulling apart his kingdom'.[5] Ominously, from the moment of his succession he believed he would be the last king of Laos.[6]

American support for the CDNI reflected the growing view that a 'Neutral' Laos would be vulnerable to a Communist takeover. At the time of the Geneva Accords, which Washington did not ratify but pledged to follow, the Americans were optimistic because Laos would be neutral in the Cold War, and there appeared no reason for the Communists to interfere. A Défense Department intelligence report on 10 June 1955 noted Laos had a sparse, rural and apathetic population, which meant revolutionary ideas based upon social and agricultural reform, such as in China and Vietnam, were unlikely to find fertile soil because there were no major social, economic or political grievances. But, the State and Défense Departments remained wary, with the LPF electoral victory sounding alarm bells.

Economic aid was the most significant aspect of American support but was based upon an artificially high exchange rate of the Laotian kip to the dollar, which brought great wealth to a few, encouraged corruption and had an adverse effect upon most of the population. Indeed, corruption was one of the factors which stimulated the growth of the CDNI and, consequently, one of Phoui's earliest decisions was to devalue the kip. Washington also began to funnel military aid into the country, but as the Geneva Accords prohibited foreign military missions, except for the MMG/RGL, the usual Military Assistance and Advisory Group (MAAG) could not be created. Following a formal Laotian request, on 13 December 1954, the Défense Department created in December 1955 what was officially described as a Programs Evaluation Office (PEO) under Brigadier General Rothwell H. Brown, who had worked in South Vietnam and Pakistan. Ostensibly this was part of the civilian aid organisation and manned by himself and the five other 'civilians', all of whom were officially reservists and wore civilian clothes, but Brown reported to the Commander-in-Chief, Pacific Command (CINCPAC) and nominally operated through the MMF/RLG. It steadily expanded until, by 1958, it had 22 people, although Washington wanted it to have 60.[7] Between 1954 and 1960 Washington provided Laos with $300 million of aid, with the first major items being four Dakota transports provided in January 1956.[8] It was against this background that the conflict which wrecked the country over the next two decades would slowly evolve.

The Pathet Lao Leaders Escape

In an unsuccessful attempt to regain control of government, Phoui sacked the CDNI cabinet members on 16 December 1959, and extended the session of the National Assembly, his power base where he retained friends and influence, beyond its scheduled 25 December closure until the elections scheduled for April 1960. But, on Christmas Eve (24 December), and with tacit CIA support, Phoumi turned the tables and on the pretext of an imminent Pathet Lao attack used troops, led by Captain Kong Le's BP 2, to take over the city with the aim of creating a 'directed democracy'. Phoui waited five days before offering his resignation, and insisted that the National Assembly remain in control until the April elections, but Phoumi closed the Assembly and the king accepted Phoui's resignation on New Year's Eve. The king was a tacit supporter of Phoumi, whom he now opted for premier, but this created a storm of opposition from Western governments and while Phoumi temporarily retained power, the coup leader now informed the king that he now looked forward to the establishment of a civilian government following the elections.[9]

The elections of 24 April proved a farce, with the fragmentation of Laotian politics thwarting American hopes that the anti-Communist parties would form an alliance. The election law was amended, effectively banning most Left-Wing candidates while the CDNI candidates had the support of the FAR, the Americans and the Thais and many of their potential opponents were bribed to withdraw. The Americans again provided air support to assist civic action programmes in northern Laos. The air support was organised by the Okinawa-based 1045th Operations, Evaluation and Training Group and in addition to using CAT's successor, Air America, it borrowed USAF C-130 Hercules transports.[10] Air America even flew village chiefs from north Phong Saly to polling centres in Luang Prabang. In southern Laos, the Army actively participated in the elections and were ordered to consult with, but not coerce, village chiefs and AD leaders regarding their election choices. The CDNI won 34 of the 59 seats, votes for their candidates often exceeding the size of the constituency electorate, the anti-Communist Rally for the Lao People (Lao Huam Lao) won 17 seats and independents won the remainder. The CDNI then created on 12 May the Social Democratic Party (Paksa Sangkhom), which formed the new government under Prince Somsanit Vongkotrattana, but he was a mouthpiece with real power in the hands of Phoumi (who remained Defence Minister) and Foreign Minister Phagna Khamphan Panya.

Both were determined to ally their country more firmly with the United States and planned to put Souphanouvong on trial. But on 23 May 1960, a fortnight before the government was formed, Souphanouvong and the other 15 imprisoned Pathet Lao leaders, together with most of their prison guards, escaped from the Phon Kheng jail in the middle of the Military Police headquarters. This was a tremendous success for a North Vietnamese Intelligence team, headed by Phan Dinh who had supervised clandestine operations inside Vientiane during the war against the French. After months of coercion, persuasion, bribes, and exploiting family ties, he was able to organise the breakout with the politicians escorted by Pathet Lao troops disguised as police to safe houses and hideouts.[11] They then marched eastwards through the jungle for 500 kilometres, reaching Sam Neua four months later. By now the Pathet Lao regarded the election as confirmation that Washington was trying to turn Laos into a colony or a protectorate, and began demanding an American withdrawal.

The new strongman in Laos was General Phoumi Nosavan, who held the post of Defence Minister as well as being the Commander-in-Chief of the FAL. On 25 December 1959, he led a bloodless coup which installed the CDNI in power. (Albert Grandolini Collection)

Once again, tanks in the streets of Bangkok. On 16 September 1957, Thailand's Field Marshal Thanarat Sarit launched a coup which ousted the Phibun government. (Albert Grandolini Collection)

Field Marshal Thanarat Sarit was a first cousin of the Lao new strongman, Phoumi Nosavan. He fully backed him to blunt any advance of communism in Laos. (Albert Grandolini Collection)

Succeeding his father, the popular King Sisavang Vong, the new king Savang Vatthana was enthroned on 29 October 1959. Prophetically, he stated that he would be the last king of Laos. After the communists took over in 1975, he was deported into a re-education camp where he died of starvation, together with Queen Kamphoui and one of his sons, Prince Vong Savang. (Albert Grandolini Collection)

The massive uncontrolled US aid to Laos accelerated the fracturing of the country, fuelling the corruption of the warring elites. It also caused a widening gap between the living conditions in the main urban centres, like here in Vientiane, with a fictitious prosperity and the impoverished countryside. All of this fuelled communist propaganda and enrolment. (Albert Grandolini Collection)

From Demobilisation to Mobilisation

During 1959 Laos became increasingly polarised through a combination of personal ambition, revolutionary determination and international realpolitik, dashing hopes of a political solution creating the neutral country sought by the 1954 Geneva Accords.

The growing insurgency in South Vietnam created a further complication, for Hanoi's decision to create a logistical supply system to the South Vietnamese insurgents, the so-called Ho Chi Minh Trail, would turn much of the Panhandle into a North Vietnamese protectorate. Hanoi's decision and Washington's determination to prevent a Communist take-over turned the country into a proxy battleground between North Vietnam and the United States.

The ICC had monitored the first steps towards merging the ANL and Pathet Lao (PL) forces, 60 days after the establishment of a coalition government in an arrangement giving all fighters uniform benefits including pensions. A ceremony of token assimilation by Pathet Lao forces on the Plain of Jars took place in February 1958, but they then demanded 105 of their officers be included in the ANL, and it was not until April 1959 that the government conceded the point, with the proviso that all candidates first pass a written examination. In the meantime, the Pathet Lao troops in the Plain of Jars were divided into two battalions and, while 2nd PL Battalion remained in their original camp, the 1st PL Battalion was transferred to Xieng Ngeun, 14 kilometres southeast of Luang Prabang.[12]

All obstacles to the formal integration on 11 May 1959 now appeared overcome, and on 7 May the new ANL Chief-of-Staff, Brigadier Ouane Rathikoun, decided to visit the 1st Battalion. But the Pathet Lao, instead of meeting their new commander with honours as Ouane would have expected, were alarmed about the growing influence of anti-Communists in Vientiane and aimed their weapons at him, forcing him to return to Vientiane. The furious general ordered three battalions in the vicinity of the encampment to surround it and, on 10 May, gave the Pathet Lao 24 hours to line up for the integration ceremony.

The 1st Battalion agreed to the ceremony on 17 May 1959, as did their comrades the following day, but on the night of 10/11 May, under cover of heavy rain, the 2nd Battalion infiltrated through the ANL lines and began a forced march alongside Route 4 to the high ground southeast of the plain. Ouane ordered BI 25 to pursue them down Route 4 while, to head them off, a BP 2 company dropped at Tha Thom, but many paratroopers fell ill with malaria and after a month were withdrawn. The Pathet Lao had already turned east heading for North Vietnam and on 22 May they reached Moung Ngan, as PAVN's 4th Military Region sent a detachment across the border to shield them. The Pathet Lao's 'pursuers' showed a marked lack of enthusiasm and Ouane now committed BI 10 under a Hmong officer, Major Vang Pao, who intercepted the enemy at Moung Ngan only to run out of ammunition. This allowed the Pathet Lao to escape into North Vietnam, although Hmong members under Lieutenant Colonel Thao Tou Saychou remained along the Houa Phan/Xieng Khouang provincial boundary north of Ban Ban. Ouane sacked Major Sang Kittirath for allowing the enemy to escape and replaced him with Lieutenant Colonel Khamkhong Bouddavong, who would soon face a new crisis. Meanwhile, the 1st PL Battalion in Xieng Nguen was split between those who wished to accept integration and those opposed, and on the night of 8/9 August a hundred of the opponents left their barracks and began marching northeast. The remaining 375 men were transferred to Vientiane on 15 August, and then sent by boat down the Mekong to Saravane to fill out a RM-4 battalion.

Meanwhile, a newly created PAVN advisory/assistance organisation, Group 800, reorganised the 2nd PL Battalion into the 1st, 2nd, and 3rd Battalions, while the Pathet Lao main force was reorganised into five battalions by the end of 1959, each with a North Vietnamese advisory team and signal platoon. Some battalions were filled-out with North Vietnamese draftees, while the 3rd Battalion consisted entirely of North Vietnamese 'Internationalist Volunteers'.[13] Kaysone now ordered bases re-established within Houa Phan and in July 1959 the Pathet Lao began crossing the border in the north and northeast of the province. Within a fortnight, four FAL outposts were either stormed or abandoned leaving most of the province under Pathet Lao control. Vientiane's administrator Khong, now

After escaping from jail with other Pathet Loa ministers, Souphanouvong finally reached the safety of North Vietnam where he inspected Pathet Lao troops. Soon, he would resume hostilities with Vientiane. (Albert Grandolini Collection)

The Pathet Lao 2nd Battalion was also earmarked to be integrated into the ANL and is seen here on their regrouping station in the Plain of Jars. It broke through the government lines, on 10 May 1959, to reach safety in North Vietnam. (Albert Grandolini Collection)

In an unsuccessful attempt to intercept the PL 2 Battalion, it was decided to drop a company of BP 2 at Tha Tom. The paratroopers are seen here boarding a C-47 under watchful eyes of French advisors. (Albert Grandolini Collection)

On 7 May 1959, the new ANL Chief-of Staff, Brigadier Ouane Rathikoun, was unceremoniously turned back at gunpoint by the troops of the Pathet Lao 1st Battalion stationed at Xieng Nguen, starting a new crisis which saw a renewal of fighting with the Communists. He is seen here, at right, with new King Savang Vatthana. (Albert Grandolini Collection)

promoted to Lieutenant Colonel, moved three companies towards the border and they retook two of the posts on 28 July. Vientiane also decided to impose its authority in Houa Phan by strengthening the provincial AD forces with BP 2, while FAL Deputy Chief-of-Staff Brigadier Amkha Soukhavong was flown in to re-establish control along the Vietnam border.

While BP 2 was nominally under Major Sisamouth Sananikone, the driving force within it was his deputy commander Major Kong Le, who was Lao Theong/Kha, and sent two companies to the border where they encountered no resistance. But when Kong Le drove into Sam Neua on 1 August to brief Amkha, he was shocked to discover all the troops and officials had fled the town that morning for the 'safety' of former AD stronghold Moung Peun. The following morning Phoumi and Ouane flew in, ordered Amkha in no uncertain terms to return to his post and reinforced him with most of BI 4 from Attopeu and a company from BI 26, the latter made up of former Pathet Lao troops. To help RM-2 focus upon the task, they placed Vientiane under Phoumi's new RM-5, while the truncated region's headquarters was moved to Long Tieng in Xieng Khouang.

The resurgence of the Right in Laos came as a shock to Hanoi, but it was the May 1959 crisis which proved the turning point. In early May the VWP Politburo and Central Committee met to discuss the situation and concluded that supporting the Pathet Lao was essential to supporting the 'liberation' of South Vietnam. The Vietnamese and Pathet Lao met at Xuan Thanh in Nghe An province to hammer out a response and, on 3 June, concluded the Americans were the prime threat. On 6 July 1959, a Working Committee on Laos was created under Vo Nguyen Giap, with Vietnamese experts including Nguyen Khang. To direct military and political operations within Laos, Group 959 was created in September under Brigadier Nguyen Throng Vinh with 88 personnel at Na Kai in Houa Phan, to command Vietnamese 'volunteer' units within the country while also having a subsidiary mission to expand the Pathet Lao forces. The VWP Western Party Affairs Committee, renamed the Western Regional Working Committee, and including Chuy Huy Man, was attached to Group 959 to oversee its operations.[14]

PAVN reversed the demobilisations of the previous years and prepared to support Group 959, with Vinh responsible for strategy and political questions. The Northwest and 4th Military Regions were responsible for executing military operations and their logistical support. The 316th Brigade in the Moc Chau Highlands was now to control battalion-sized operations in Laos, with elements of the 174th and 176th Infantry augmented by units from 280th and 673rd Infantry Regiments. In central Laos, north of the 17th Parallel, the 4th Region deployed the 148th Independent Infantry's 910th, 920th and 930th Battalions, with the 270th Regiment's 263rd Battalion, while in Khammouane Province were elements of the 120th Infantry.[15]

During the second half of August the Pathet Lao began expanding deeper into the province and now contested control of the border regions, leading to minor clashes with FAL forces, and PEO organised a drop by CAT of 50 BP 1 troops into Moung Peun to shield the growing AD force, air support being provided by Air America/CAT. On 30 August 1959, the North Vietnamese 3rd PL Battalion joined the battle and the FAL troops fled back to Sam Neua, but the Communists did not try to follow up this success and an uneasy peace returned. The Pathet Lao now firmly controlled Phong Saly, with their 2nd and 4th Battalions around Xieng Khuoang, while the 1st Battalion held the area north of Route 8 and Route 12.[16] On 19 August, the US Joint Chiefs of Staff estimated in JCM-580-60 the Pathet Lao had 2,500/3,000 main force and 5,500/6,000 local force troops with limited transport facilities, weapons and ammunition.

The Pathet Lao now benefitted from years of cultivating the minorities to fuel expansions in Phong Saly, Xieng Khouang and Luang Prabang. In Phong Saly, Faidang Lobliayao, a well-respected Hmong clan leader who had thrown in his lot with the Viet Minh against the French, was now a vice-president of the Lao Patriotic Front.[17] He led a third of the province's Hmong and was reinforced by Tais, some from North Vietnam, and slowly but steadily extended his control. In the Panhandle, Sithon Kammadam reactivated the Lao Theung networks which attacked outposts and began to control roads. By 1960 the Pathet Lao claimed to control 20 percent of the country's population in almost every province, with government control in some provinces restricted to a 20 kilometre area around the capital.[18] In late October 1960, Pathet Lao/PAVN troops overran San Louang, 47 kilometres east of Attopeu in RM-4, to control the key junction of Routes 96 and 110 as part of a process of extending the Ho Chi Minh Trail into Laos.

In July 1959, the PAVN 316th Brigade received orders to redeploy toward the Laotian border, before crossing on foot into Laos. Leading a column of ZIS-150 lorries on a pontoon bridge is a GAZ-67 command car. (PAVN)

Supporting the Pathet Lao, these Vietnamese officers of the PAVN 270th Regiment redeploy their troops to attack a Laotian outpost in Khammouane Province in August 1959. (PAVN)

A North Vietnamese crew of an 75mm M20 recoilless rifle is preparing to fire against a Laotian outpost in Moung Peun area in support of a Pathet Lao attack. (PAVN)

BP 2 was dropped into Sam Nuea area, trying to stem the Pathet Lao advance. The unit was then used as a fire brigade, being constantly deployed to any threatened sectors, without much rest between two operations. (Albert Grandolini Collection)

The attack continues with the support of FM-24/29 LMG. At that date, most of the Pathet Lao equipment was of French origin. (PAVN)

A crew-served MAC-31A2 machine gun covering a Pathet Lao assault against a FAL outpost in Houa Phan Province in August 1959. (PAVN)

A group of Pathet Lao soldiers in an ambush position during the summer of 1959 in Xieng Khuoang area. (PAVN)

Reinforcements were poured into Sam Neua by Civil Air Transport and Air America aircraft to reinforce the local garrison. By September 1959, an equivalent of a regiment was deployed there. (Albert Grandolini Collection)

Sam Nuea became the focal point for Anti-Communist activity and in the face of the North Vietnamese advance most of the region's Self-Défense AD concentrated there. (Albert Grandolini Collection)

The French-trained Lao Intelligence, the National Documentation Centre (Centre National de Documentation) or CND, sent radio-equipped teams, each of six agents, on foot into the Pathet Lao-held areas of Xieng Khouang, Houa Phou, Thakhek and Savannakhet in July, replacing those killed or captured. They were augmented between August and September by three teams parachuted into Xieng Kho, Muong Sone, and Samteu in Houa Phou, while two were dropped at Muong Ngoi and Pakseng in Luang Prabang. In December, additional teams were parachuted in the north and northwest sectors of the Vientiane Province to assess communist activities at Muong Ngoi and the right bank of the Nam Ma River. On 19 January, another two teams were dropped into Sop Bao and Sop Hao, northeast of Sam Nuea, to report on North Vietnamese cross-border activity at Moc Chau and Hoi Xuan.[19]

Vientiane's justified claims of a PAVN presence were subject to an unsuccessful four-week United Nations investigation in late September, but SEATO, whose military advisors met at a scheduled conference on September 20, were more pessimistic. Asian members pressed for intervention, but the non-Asian members preferred to wait and see as the geographic problems of intervention were formidable. Nevertheless, on 7 September US Joint Task Force 116 (JTF 116) was assigned two attack and one anti-submarine carrier groups to support potential intervention, while South Korea's President Syngman Rhee made a secret offer to deploy two divisions into Laos. When the crisis abated, President Eisenhower on 11 September decided to intervene only if Vientiane requested SEATO's help, and disbanded JTF 116 while Washington decided to fund an expansion of the FAL to 29,000 as well as temporarily to finance 4,000 guerrillas in Houa Phan province.[20]

The resurgence of the Pathet Lao stimulated a renaissance in mid-1959 of the AD programme abandoned in 1958.[21] The original concept was for a village self-defence militia of 100-man companies, later Auto-Défense Ordinaire (Ordinary Self Defence), who would form the majority of the troops, but in some areas full-time companies were formed to take a more active role against the Pathet Lao as Auto-Défense de Choc (Shock Self Defence) or ADC, training and support being the responsibility of the regional BVs. By the beginning of September, the 16,000 men were being trained and there were plans to add another 4,000 by the end of October.

The low-level conflict continued through the first half of 1960, but it was clear that with CDNI's April election victory and Souphanouvong rejoining his Pathet Lao comrades, the country was drifting into full-scale war. It was also clear that US economic aid was actually helping to create the problem by feeding inflation and widening the gap between the urban elite and the rural poor.[22]

Table 4-1: AD distribution on 1 September 1959

Military Region	Province (BV)	AD strength
RM-1	Phong Saly (BV 11)	2,100
	Nam Tha (BV 13)	500
	Luang Prabang (BV 12)	2,000
	Sayaboury (BV 14)	400
RM-2	Xieng Khouang (BV 21)	1,800
	Houa Phou (BV 23)	1,900
RM-3	Khammouane (BV 32)	1,765
	Savannakhet (BV 31)	1,235
RM-4	Pakse (BV 42)	1,100
	Saravane (BV 41)	1,000
	Attopeu (BV 43)	900
RM-5	Vientiane (BV 22)	1,300
Source: Conboy/Morrison p.23, 29 n.65		

Left: In addition to the military FAL Intelligence Department, funded by the PEO and the CIA, the Laotian government also relied on French-trained Lao Intelligence, the National Documentation Centre (Centre National de Documentation) or CND. In 1959, it sent several radio-equipped teams behind communist lines to gather information. One of its agents, in civilian clothes, is seen here armed with an M3 SMG. (Albert Grandolini Collection)

Right: In September 1959, for four weeks a United Nations investigation team arrived in Laos when Vientiane accused North Vietnam of preparing to invade its territory. The team settled in Sam Neua, being flown there on board RLAF and Air America C-47s. (United Nations archives)

The CND teams were usually air supported by contracted local airlines, such as Air Laos, but mostly by Veha Akat. A small group of selected French civilian pilots worked with that airline and were privy to such special operations with the CND or the French SDCE Intelligence. They used a motley collection of DC-3s and DHC-2 Beavers to drop agents or supplies. (Albert Grandolini Collection)

The UN inspection team, made up of representatives from Argentina, Italy, and Tunisia, arrived in Sam Nuea. Using Beaver light aircraft, they also visited Sam Teu and other smaller settlements. (United Nations archives)

For the rest of 1959, low-level fighting continued around Sam Nuea held by BI 4, BI 6, BP 2, artillery, and an armoured troop with M5 Stuart light tanks, M8 Greyhound armoured cars, and half-tracks. Most of the fighting was northeast of the town. (Albert Grandolini Collection)

A troop of M5 Stuart light tanks was held at Sam Nuea in reserve for local counterattacks if the situation required it. (Albert Grandollnl Collection)

A FAL M5 Stuart tank guarding a crossroad at the entrance to Sam Nuea in 1959. (Leif Hellstrom Collection)

One of the FAL outposts covering Sam Nuea seen in October 1959. Many of them were already encircled by the Pathet Lao and were resupplied only by air. (Albert Grandolini Collection)

A group of Pathet Lao prisoners is presented to the United Nations inspection team in October 1959 as a proof of North Vietnamese aggression. They informed the inspectors that their commanding officers were from PAVN. (Albert Grandolini Collection)

Increased American involvement

Since 1958 Washington's concern about Laotian ability to resist 'communist aggression' had been growing. In May 1958 the Défense Department proposed specialist training for ANL troops and sent some engineer instructors, while in October it organised training for 39 officers and non-commissioned officers at infantry and airborne schools at Fort Benning, Georgia. But the PEO now assumed a major role following the appointment in September 1958 of Brigadier John A. Heintges as its director.[23]

German-born Heintges had a distinguished career, which would end as Deputy Commander of the Korea-based 8th Army, and from November 1965 to May 1967 he would be Deputy Commander of the Military Assistance Command, Vietnam (MACV), being succeeded by General Creigthon W. Abrams. He arrived in Vientiane in November 1958 to begin a root-and-branch review of PEO's activities known as the Heintges Plan. He concluded objectives were too limited, essentially being a logistical organisation delivering US equipment for distribution by the MAAF/RLG with no idea how it was used, indeed there were suspicions some was reaching Algeria. He noted the FAL officers had little in common with the rank-and-file, non-commissioned officers were poorly educated and trained, while there was an endemic shortage of modern equipment. He proposed greater control over the distribution of US equipment and the PEO assume responsibility for FAL training.

The proposals were accepted, and in December the PEO was expanded to 65, many of them, like Heintges, wartime veterans of the 3rd Infantry Division. The French initially opposed American attempts to muscle-into their training responsibilities, but in May 1959 these were split with the French continuing to provide tactical training while the Americans provided 'technical' training involving newly delivered US equipment. Paris also agreed the Americans could deploy up to 120 more instructors on six-month tours which could be renewed for six months. In July Vientiane, encouraged by Washington, requested increased military aid with direct American training, which provided an opportunity for the Green Berets, as the US Special Forces were called soon after their formation in June 1952. Logically, this would have involved the 1st Special Forces Group based on Okinawa from June 1957, because it is about a thousand nautical miles from potential conflict sites in eastern and south-eastern Asia and was training in South Vietnam.[24] But CINCPAC opted instead to use the 77th Special Forces Group (7th Group from June 6), based in Fort Bragg, North Carolina.[25]

On 22 January it was ordered to provide a dozen eight-man Mobile Training Teams (MTT) under Lieutenant Colonel Arthur D. 'Bull' Simons as Project 'Hotfoot'. The Green Berets arrived in civilian clothes at Wattay on 24 July, with the 22-man B (Control) Team deployed to Vientiane and the training teams to rear-area sites at Luang Prabang, Vientiane, Savannakhet and Pakse as part of the PEO's Laotian Training Advisory Group, working with the MMF/RLG from September, but beginning the process of reducing French influence.

The men were on six-months temporary duty tours which reduced the impact, for no sooner were they familiar with the Laotians, than they were replaced in January 1960 by 'Hotfoot II', whose men then had to relearn the lessons as did 'Hotfoot III' which arrived in July 1960, contravening the agreement with the French.[26] In addition, during 1959 several US Naval Mobile Construction Battalions (Seabees) detachments improved strategically important roads and the Wattay Airbase.[27] Fighting in the east delayed training efforts in the use of Second World War vintage weapons until September, but gave the Americans time to take the measure of their hosts. To provide further support the PEO requested CINCPAC provide six more transports for the FAL, two Dakotas and four Beavers.

Simultaneously, the PEO was expanded and by the end of the year was authorised 175 full-duty, 190 contracted and 149-temporary duty personnel, of whom 428 were in country by the beginning of 1960. They were by augmented in January by 103 Filipinos, who formed the Manila-based Eastern Construction Company (ECCOIL) in Laos. These men, ostensibly engineers, were all veterans of guerrilla warfare in the Philippines, with the company contracted to provide technical training for the army and act as instructors to Lao air and naval forces, but it also provided military and paramilitary advisors to Asian countries.[28] Buddhist Thailand, angered by the suppression of Tibetan Buddhist culture by China, and fearful of Communist expansion during 1959, resumed training links with Laos after a two-year break, with Sarit arranging counter-insurgency training courses for Laotian paratroopers.

In response to the crisis in eastern Laos, CINCPAC prepared Operations Plan 32-59 in which Major General Carson A. Roberts' JTF 116, with three carrier task groups earmarked on 7 September, would secure airheads at Vientiane and Seno allowing the FAL to focus upon the Communist threat. The task force was activated at Iwakuni Airbase, Japan, on 15 August, and as Roberts also commanded the 1st Marine Aircraft Wing in Japan, he was assigned Marine Air Group 12 (MAG 12) and the 9th Marine Infantry Regiment while he went on an inspection tour of Laos.[29]

The PEO decided to reshuffle the FAL training system after the renewal of hostilities in 1959 by deploying more American instructors who were charged to supplement, then replace, the French advisors. It was decided to introduce US Army Special Forces instructors with Project 'Hotfoot' under Lt Col Arthur D. Simons, a veteran of Ranger special operations in the Pacific during the Second World War. (US Army)

Green Berets of Project 'Hotfoot' began training Laotian troops to use American equipment and weapons in joint training camps with French advisors at Luang Prabang, Vientiane, Savannakhet, and Pakse. They also built a new facility northeast of Vientiane, without French participation, and eventually that was where most of the training was concentrated. (US Army)

For the time being both the American PEO and the French MMF/RLG formally accepted the delineation between the two training missions in their assigned tasks. To the Americans the technical instruction of the Laotian troops, to the French the tactical training. A French advisor seen in the streets of Vientiane in 1960. (Albert Grandolini Collection)

5

HANOI'S FATEFUL DECISION

A key decision was also made in Hanoi in September 1959. Following the Geneva Conference, the Viet Minh moved most of their personnel, some 90,000, from south of the 17th Parallel, Laos and Cambodia into North Vietnam, leaving a skeleton force of cadres born south of the Parallel for low-level political work.[1] They returned to help the VWP rebuild the country and improve land reform, which the Party had botched. On 5 September 1954, the Central Committee's Politburo opted for a two-nation solution, with those in the south ordered to focus upon the political struggle (dau tranh chinh tri) rather than armed struggle (dau tranh). This was also emphasised in the June 1956 resolution about the future of South Vietnam's revolution and in an 18 August 1956 letter to the southern Party leadership (The 1956 resolution had the proviso: '...this does not mean...that we will never employ self-defence measures in limited situations').[2]

Diem's success in consolidating power in South Vietnam wrecked the Party organisation and drove the surviving VWP members into sanctuaries within the Mekong Delta, western South Vietnam and in the Highlands, where they created 'self-defence' units, although they continued to focus upon political activity. Sheer survival forced what their foes called 'Vietnamese Communists' (Viet Nam Cong San) or Viet Cong, to use their 'self-defence' units more actively. The Communists exploited peasant grievances to extend their influence aided by armed propaganda units who began eliminating all local opposition as the bases slowly expanded.

Some VWP leaders, notably Premier Pham Van Dong, publicly advocated peaceful reunification, but having restored stability to North Vietnam by the end of 1958 the Party faced growing demands for support from the south, who sent representatives to the Central Committee's 15th plenary session in January 1959. Partly because of growing American influence in Laos, the VWP decided to overthrow the 'imperialist and feudalist' southern regime and prepared to support 'a protracted armed struggle'.[3] The General Military Party Committee was ordered to direct the expansion of southern base areas and to deploy the PAVN to support the forces in the south, Pham Van Dong informing a Western diplomat: 'We will drive the Americans into the sea'.[4] This confidence was boosted by the success of a series of divisional-size exercises conducted during 1958, including one by the 335th Brigade re-trained in jungle mountain warfare '...to prepare themselves to return to the battlefields of Laos to carry out their international duties'.[5]

Creating the Ho Chi Minh Trail

On the morning of 19 May 1959, Ho Chi Minh's birthday, PAVN logistics specialist and Deputy Director of the Army Agricultural Farms Department, Colonel Vo Bam, was summoned to the offices of the Central Military Committee. There he met Major General Nguyen Van Vinh, Deputy Defence Minister and head of Personnel, who informed him he was to create a supply line to the south as a conduit for troops, captured French weapons and supplies. He was not allowed to keep written records and was directly under the Military Committee with no more than 500 men. Post-war Vietnamese accounts claim that Vo Bam was told the Trail would be within Vietnam's borders and across the Demilitarised Zone (DMZ), areas where he served with the Viet Minh. But, it was obvious that it would have to go through Laos, and to organise the moves south he created the 301st Land Transportation Battalion using men from Colonel Nguyen Minh Chau's 305th Brigade, which had once operated in the Panhandle. General Tran Luong, who was a 'southerner', was selected to organise the Viet Cong's military expansion, which would become the National Liberation Army and, when he briefed Bam, told him: 'The route must be kept absolutely secret. It must not be allowed to become a beaten path...not a single footprint, cigarette butt or broken twig may be left on it after the men's passage'.[6]

The 338th Division, consisting of southern regroupees, was converted into a re-training unit for troops sent south supported by the Northwest and 4th Military Regions.[7] The first 'agitation-propaganda' teams, totalling 300 men, departed on 10 June, arriving on 20 August, using a trail the Viet Minh had built through the mountains along the western frontier with Laos, but on the Vietnamese side of the border. On 19 May 1959, Vo Bam's command was redesignated Transportation Group 559 (the date it was established) with its

The reason Hanoi re-started war in Laos in 1959 was because of the decision to intervene directly in the South Vietnam insurgency. PAVN Transportation Group 559 was charged in great secrecy to open a logistic corridor along the Truong Son (Annamite) mountains range to infiltrate men and weapons to the South through southern Laos. (PAVN)

The first infiltrated troops into South Vietnam were former Viet Minh southerners who had been evacuated to North Vietnam after the Geneva Accords of 1954. Most came from the PAVN 338th Division, consisting of southern regroupees, armed mostly with French-made weapons to conceal the fact the troops had been sent by Hanoi. (PAVN)

There were several projects between South Vietnam and Laos to conduct joint military operations along Route 9 in order to interdict North Vietnamese infiltration. As early as 1958 the South Vietnamese Special Advisor to President Ngo Dinh Diem, his brother Ngo Dinh Nhu, visited Vientiane to discuss the issue. However, none saw fruition although this picture shows South Vietnamese and Laotian troops shaking hands at the border mark on Route 9 in 1959. (Albert Grandolini Collection)

headquarters in Ly Dam De Street, Hanoi, and two transport units; the 301st Land and 603rd Sea Transportation Battalions, the latter with 107 men, but it soon became clear establishing the trail would create problems greater than anticipated.[8] Also in May, the North Vietnamese Communist Party's 15th Plenum ordered the establishment of an overall command for political and military activities in South Vietnam, originally called the National Assembly Reunification Committee, in 1961, but renamed in 1962 the Central Office in South Vietnam (Van Phong Trung Uong Cục Mien Nam) or COSVN, in South Vietnam's Tay Ninh Province. Both Vientiane and Saigon swiftly became aware of the infiltration and began patrolling Route 9 on each side of the border, the former covering a 12 kilometre stretch of the road while the latter concentrated around Ban Houei Sane just inside Laos, where the South Vietnamese also established a special forces unit. To counter the infiltration, Washington proposed creating an all-weather road from Kontum in Vietnam across southern Laos, past Attopeu and around the Bolovens Plateau but Diem was not interested in the US$6 million plan, which was too expensive, and it was abandoned in October.[9]

The Kong Le Coup

The polarisation of the nation, together with government ineptitude and foreign interference, troubled BP 2's commander, Kong Le. A naïve but contemplative man who distrusted Washington and Bangkok's claims that Laos faced Communist subversion, believing them excuses to interfere in Laotian affairs. He also believed the Laotian people were essentially peaceful and could end the conflict. He wished to see a truly neutral Laos and discussed his ideas with fellow officers, politicians such as Souvanna Phouma, as well as the French including Jean Deuve, Premier Phoui's Special Political Advisor as well as SDCE's head-of-station. When Kong Le asked Deuve about France's position on Laotian neutrality the response came directly from President de Gaulle on 11 February 1959, confirming French support.[10] Kong Le also had grievances over the poor treatment of his men when they deployed into Houa Phan and Amkha's desertion. His disquiet grew when, in March, his battalion was flown to Attopeu province to meet a surge in Pathet Lao activity and requests for air supply drops were ignored, followed by the futile attempt to catch Soupahouvong which saw so many of his men fall sick.

He crossed the Rubicon and began planning a coup to take Vientiane using his own paratroopers, some armour, and elements of BI 25 as well as air force personnel. The catalyst was an order on 8 August to make a sweep along Route 13 north of Vientiane. The men were angry about constant deployment and their pay being two months in arrears, and on that same day most senior government figures, including the Premier, the Cabinet and almost all the generals (except Amkha and RM commander Sing Rattanasamy) flew to Luang Prabang to arrange the cremation of King Sisavong Vong. The overstrength battalion, 842 men, had just conducted an exercise involving the occupation of a city with emphasis upon taking the radio station, and this provided a template for the coup.[11]

Before dawn on 9 August, Kong Le seized Vientiane, arrested FAL commander General Sounthone Patbammavong and appointed Souvanna Phouma the new Premier. Kong Le's broadcast railed against government corruption and foreign influences, and his direct way of speaking appealed to many listeners. To thwart political opposition, on 13 August, his troops, and a noisy crowd of supporters, surrounded the National Assembly, where the 41 remaining deputies passed a vote of no-confidence in Phoui's government. Four days later the assembly approved the new Souvanna government, and the monarch graciously accepted the *fait accompli*, allowing Kong Le's troops to return to barracks.

The ministers in Luang Prabang were stunned by the coup, but on 10 August Phoumi flew to Thailand to meet his cousin Sarit and seek support for a countercoup. While the Thai strongman feared the Kong Le's actions might expand Communist influence within Laos, he refused to commit himself and Phoumi returned to Savannkhet on 12 August empty-handed. There he received the support of the RM-3 and RM-4 commanders, Colonels Bounphone Marthepharak and Phasouk Somly Rasphakdi, giving him a secure base, while RM-2 commander Colonel Khamkhong Bouddavong was already a supporter. Two days later he brought most of the government ministers and deputies to Savannkhet as the first step in the countercoup, and created a Counter Coup d'État Committee (CCEC). But, for the moment, the conflict was waged only on the air waves, the Pathet Lao joining in on Kong Le's side from 19 August, and on 24 August announcing their support for Souvanna Phouma.

In late August, Souvanna and General Ouane flew to Seno to negotiate with Phoumi, leading to a new government on 30 August, with Ouane appointed Commander-in-Chief and Phoumi as Interior Minister while the CCEC was disbanded. The National Assembly met in Luang Prabang, where the king approved the new Cabinet who were to take their oath of office on 2 September. But, on that day Kong Le made a series of anti-Phoumi broadcasts which so offended the general he returned to Savannakhet, and refused to implement the agreement, then he reformed the CCEC on 10 September, assured he would receive US support.

Foreign Reaction

Kong Le's neutralist policy, and his links with the Pathet Lao, confirmed Washington's worst fears. Some in the Administration wanted to support the Laotian government while others wanted to support the Neutralists, including a junior foreign service officer called William H. Sullivan whose idea was to give each political group its own part of Laos. Within the country, Ambassador Winthrop G. Brown, who arrived only on 25 July, supported Souvanna Phouma, but the Deputy PEO commander, Colonel Albert Brownfield, moved to Savannakhet to back Phoumi with a 40-man 'shadow PEO'.[12] President Eisenhower was nearing the end of his term and did not wish to impose his policy upon his successor, but there was a growing feeling that Kong Le would align himself to the Pathet Lao. On 11 August, JTF 116 was reactivated, and the 7th Fleet deployed two carrier task forces and an amphibious group into the South China Sea to demonstrate American support for its South East Asian friends.[13]

To assess the situation, the State Department sent its Eastern Secretary of State for Far Eastern Affairs, J. Graham Parsons, to Vientiane. It was an unfortunate choice for, although Parsons was a career diplomat and had been ambassador in Laos between October 1956 to February 1958, he and Souvanna Phouma disliked each other. When Parsons arrived, he discovered the Laotian premier had not only opened discussions with the Pathet Lao but also planned to re-establish diplomatic relations with the Soviet Union, broken off in 1957, yet he was still requesting US military aid for Kong Le. As a result, Washington quietly informed him that he should not expect any further American military assistance, so his only option was to come to some arrangement with the Communists.

When Parsons returned to Washington, he proposed the overthrow of Souvanna, to which both the State and Défense Departments agreed. Ambassador Brown was allowed to renew US civilian aid to the new government, but only in return for permission to send military aid to Savannakhet for use against the Pathet Lao. Air America was to supply Phoumi's forces, who were reinforced by 200 Thai-trained paratroopers, and in late September the airline flew in boxes of US dollars so Phoumi could buy influence. Privately, Washington told Souvanna not to expect any more US military assistance, but he now had the promise of Soviet military aid and on 9 November announced his new cabinet, which included a Left-Wing Interior Minister, Quinim Pholsena, and two Pathet Lao representatives. His apparent drift Leftwards continued, including recognising the People's Republic of China on 17 November and sending 'goodwill missions' to Hanoi and Beijing. The following day, he publicly announced his government would accept Pathet Lao members, and the two sides agreed he would lead a tripartite government from which Phoumi was naturally excluded and, in addition, that Laos would accept aid from China and North Vietnam.

The changes reflected the Soviet Union's surprise intervention. Relations with China were so strained that Moscow ended all cooperation with Beijing on producing nuclear weapons, with all the Soviet advisers withdrawn from China in July 1960. These actions reflected not only the deterioration of relations between the Communist super-powers but also Premier Nikita Khruschev's new policy détente with the West. When Kong Le rebelled, Ho Chi Minh was in Beijing trying to mediate in the dispute, and while China was very concerned about events in Laos, it adopted a wait-and-see policy. But, between 12-16 December Foreign Minister Zhou Enlai twice met Hanoi's Ambassador, Tran Tu Binh, to seek a joint response, and during the next year provided weapons and supplies for up to 20,000 Pathet Lao troops.[14]

Moscow saw in the Laos crisis an opportunity to assert leadership of world Communism and underline its super-power status. The Ambassador to Cambodia, Aleksandr Abramov, was now also accredited to Laos and arrived in Vientiane on 13 October to offer humanitarian, financial and military aid. Souvanna said the end of US military assistance meant the FAL lacked the resources to fight Phoumi, despite a request to the PEO for infantry weapons and ammunition to support three infantry and two paratrooper battalions. Abramov noted: 'Souvanna said this list represents the maximum and the Lao government would be happy if the Soviet government gave us half or even a-fifth of what is on the list'. Abramov promised to forward the list to Moscow.[15]

Bangkok reacted by instituting a blockade of food and fuel deliveries into Laos but, after a SEATO conference endorsed Washington's policy on Laos, it assumed a more active role. The RTA already had Headquarters 309 to define strategic policy for the country's eastern neighbours, and in late September this created a secret military advisory group to operate alongside Phoumi. Officially this was the Thai Committee to Support Laos (Khanakamkan Thai Phueatnapsanun Lao), known by its Thai acronym Kaw Taw, under Colonel Vanlop Rochanavisut, the chief of the Supreme Command's Intelligence Operations Centre. Phoumi had wanted only financial assistance and proved less than welcoming to the detachment leader, Colonel Chamnien Pongpyrot, who was never privy to his plans. Bangkok also involved the BPP's elite Police Aerial Reinforcement Unit (PARU), which was formed with CIA assistance in April 1954 originally as part of the Royal Guard but renamed in 1958 to provide the BPP with a Special Force capability. Organised into five-man, radio-equipped teams, they were trained in both insurgency and counter-insurgency operations with many recruited from frontier provinces. As early as 1956, the PARU established three intelligence-gathering posts along the Mekong and their Laotian-speaking men frequently crossed the river to assess the situation. These operations were stepped up from November 1960 among the Hmong and Kha tribes, many of whom had cousins in Thailand.[16]

While the politicians talked, Kong Le strengthened his position using two companies on 22 September to drive two pro-Phoumi battalions of out of Paksane, 120 kilometres up the Mekong from Vientiane. Having established a line along the River Kading, he turned his attention eastwards to Houa Phan where the pro-Phoumi provincial commander, Lieutenant Colonel Khong Vongnarath, had the equivalent of a regiment, 1,500 men, at Sam Neua including paratroopers and heavy mortars. The Pathet Lao had regarded Kong Le as a potential ally who would help divide their opponents, and Souphanouvong sent an emissary to meet him. On 16 September, they ordered their troops not to engage Kong Le's Neutralist forces but to concentrate upon the garrisons which had declared for Phoumi, and the following day they began to tighten their grip on Sam Neua.

On 18 September Kong Le sent some paratroopers in an Air America transport to Sam Neua to establish his authority, but Khong refused to allow them to disembark. Kong Le now dropped 20 paratroopers on Sam Neua, whereupon the garrison stampeded westwards to be rallied at Moung Peun by the regional commander, Colonel Khamkhong, and Amkha. They ordered the troops back to Sam Neua but only one battalion obeyed. They discovered the town occupied not only by Kong Le's paratroopers but also by the Pathet Lao and, more ominously, PAVN advisors, the entire battalion was taken prisoner and flown to captivity in Hanoi. Shortly afterwards RM-2 commander Colonel Khamkhong Bouddavong was invited to Vientiane for discussions, and was promptly jailed to be replaced on 7 October by Amkha. But, when Amkha flew out to take up his post he himself was arrested by the Hmong commander of BI 10, Major Vang Pao, who confirmed RM-2's loyalty to Phoumi and sent Amkha to Savannakhet, where he remained a prisoner until January 1963. Phoumi appointed Kong Le's former commander, Colonel Sourith Don Sasorith, to lead RM-2 and flew some planeloads of money and obsolete weapons to Vang Pao to ensure his loyalty.

Washington made a last-ditch diplomatic effort to find a peaceful solution, with Brown asking the King on 6 October to pressure both sides to form a caretaker government, while Parsons returned in a vain effort to persuade Souvanna Phouma to break his links with Moscow. Simultaneously, a Deputy Assistant Secretary of Défense for International Security Affairs, John N. Irwin, met Phoumi at the Thai Ubon Airbase to assure him of American support. At the beginning of October, the Défense Department ended military aid to Vientiane and a week later Parsons returned to Vientiane in a vain final effort to find a diplomatic solution. The Americans now strengthened Phoumi's countercoup, despatching \$1 million of military aid, including 10,000 tonnes of supplies and radio transmitters, which urged Neutralist officers to defect. The CIA support was organised by James W. 'Bill' Lair, who had been based in Thailand since 1951 initially organising guerrilla networks in anticipation of a Chinese invasion then helping to create PARU, which was also seeking contacts with Thai highlanders.[17]

The Pathet Lao exploited the situation by sending a wave of cadres to strengthen their organisation in Xieng Khouang Province and even Vientiane, while Kong Le distributed some 3,000 weapons to villagers around Vientiane. The Pathet Lao grip on Houa Phan tightened and their influence was extended in Phong Saly, where RM-1 commander, Colonel Houmphanh Norasing, was a covert supporter of Souvanna Phouma's government, although by mid-November he publicly supported Phoumi. The provincial chief, Lieutenant Colonel Khamouane Boupha, had displayed antipathy towards the Phoui government following the rigged April elections, and in May his men fired upon Ouane's aircraft. He was also becoming ever friendlier with his Chinese neighbours.

The CIA now took over the military operations in Laos by backing Hmong leader Vang Pao. He developed a paramilitary force that would evolve into the main contender for the Communists in Laos. A Hmong ADC is seen here in Phou Being in the spring of 1961. (Albert Grandolini Collection)

Heading the coup was Captain Kong Le, who proclaimed at an end to government corruption, accusing the United States of meddling into Laotian affairs. He reinstated Souvanna Phouma as premier and called for a true neutralist status for the country. (Albert Grandolini Collection)

With the support of Thailand and United States, a countercoup government (Counter Coup d'État Committee – CCEC) was established in Savannakhet in southern Laos under General Phoumi Nosavan and Prince Bou Oum. (Albert Grandolini Collection)

What alarmed Washington most was the fact that Kong Le entered negotiations with the Pathet Lao. On 13 October 1960, the Soviet ambassador to Cambodia, Alexander Abramov, went to Vientiane to meet Kong Le and Souvanna Phouma to promise the Neutralists economic and military aid. (Albert Grandolini Collection)

While Washington was trying to mediate between Kong Le and Phoumi Nosavan, the CIA and Thailand decided to reinforce the enemies of the Neutralists. Bangkok mobilised the Border Patrol Police's (BPP) elite Police Aerial Reinforcement Unit (PARU), which had been created with CIA assistance, and used it to send teams inside Laos for intelligence gathering and also to support guerrilla groups among the Hmong and Kha tribes. This group of PARU commandos is being trained by CIA operatives. (Albert Grandolini Collection)

The disgruntled BP 2 was constantly engaged on operations against the Pathet Lao and North Vietnamese yet was not paid for two months, leading it to march on Vientiane on 10 August 1960. (Albert Grandolini Collection)

Phoumi's Counter-Coup

With Air America flying in advisors, money and supplies, Phoumi's preparations were complete by early November, but he had to wait until the monsoon rains eased at the end of the month. His engineers used the time to improve Route 13, which would be the axis of the offensive, while in late October, PARU sent five teams across the Mekong in uniform but without insignia. One was attached to each of Phoumi's battalions and for the first time Morse signals for the Laotian forces were transmitted in Lao rather than French.[18]

Phoumi's forces were organised into three Task Forces (Groupements); Special Mobile Task Force 1 (Groupement Mobile Spécial 1 – GMS 1), under the command of Phoumi's former aide Major Siho Lamphoutacoul with three battalions, Mobile Task Force B (Groupement Mobile B- GM B) of an armoured reconnaissance squadron, commanded by Colonel Ekarath Souvannarot, Souvanna Phouma's nephew, and the reserve Tactical Task Force (Groupement Tactique – GT), with companies drawn from BP 1 and three infantry battalions together with most of the Artillery Group's batteries. US Green Berets were attached to each of the task forces. Led by Ekarath, GMB and GT were to advance along Route 13, cross the Kading River, take Paksane then isolate Vientiane, while GMS 1 sailed up the Mekong. Kong Le was seriously outnumbered, for he had only his BP 2 supported by the unreliable BI 25, plus an empty pledge of Pathet Lao support in a region where they were weak.

His isolation was demonstrated on 10 November when the Luang Prabang garrison commander, Major Bountheng Insisiengmay, seized the town in Phoumi's name, capturing Souvanna Phouma, Ouane and RM-2 commander Colonel Houmphanh Norasing, but Bountheng then allowed them to fly to Vientiane. The following day the Premier demanded the recapture of the royal capital, but the two militia companies assigned the task with the Pathet Lao, defected. Five days later, on 16 November, Ouane defected to Phoumi's side, leaving Souvanna Phouma to appoint the aging General Sounthone Pathammavong as the nominal commander of FAL.

Phoumi's countercoup began on 21 November, with Ekarath as the spearhead moving 100 kilometres in four days to take Thakhek unopposed with the Route 12 junction. RM-3 sent a battalion along Route 12 to secure the right at Khamkeut, while the rest pushed north to cross the Kading and take Paksane on 5 December, the BP 2 company defending the town having been withdraw to Vientiane. Kong Le responded by sending most of BP 2 to cover Vientiane's eastern approaches, leaving BP 3 with only 150 men in the capital under Captain Soutchay Vongsavanh, who sent half to the western suburb of Sikhay. On 5 December Soutchay allied himself with RM-5 commander Colonel Kouprasith Abhay based at FAL headquarters in the eastern suburb of Chinaimao, and two days later he and his men drove through the capital to join Kouprasith. Air America dropped two BP 1 companies ostensibly in support of Souvanna Phouma against Kong Le and, wearing white scarves, they occupied Vientiane on 8 December in the face of only the occasional rifle shot and mortar bomb, although one of these wounded Soutchay who was evacuated to Bangkok.

Kong Le promptly ordered his men, who donned red scarves, into the capital which they easily retook to force Kouprasith back to Chinaimao, where he was joined by the remainder of BP 1 which was withdrawn from GT and also parachuted in. In a desperate effort to avoid bloodshed, on 9 December Souvanna Phouma sent FAL commander General Sounthone to Chinaimao to seek a political solution and when this failed the Premier and half-a-dozen cabinet members flew to Phnom Penh. Quinim Pholsena followed on 13 December with his family and Laotian money equivalent to some $312,000. In their absence, the National Assembly passed a vote of no-confidence in Souvanna's government on 11 December and Prince Boun Oum formed a new government which was promptly recognised by Washington and Bangkok.

On 10 December Kouprasith and Phoumi secretly met near the Thai border, but it quickly became clear this was no meeting of minds and, to side-line the RM-5 commander, Phoumi appointed a loyalist, Brigadier Bounleut Sanichanh overall commander on the Vientiane front, while former RM-2 commander Colonel Khamkong Bouddavong, who had been captured in Luang Prabang, imprisoned in Vientiane then escaped on 8 December, became commander at Chinaimao. Meanwhile, GMS 1 and GT were summoned from Paksane, but it would be several days before they arrived. As a stopgap, two infantry companies from GMS 1 were sent into Thailand, driven across country and then paddled in canoes across the Mekong to reinforce the Chinaimao garrison on 11 December, by which time Phoumi's troops were only 50 kilometres away.

At the end of November 1960, the counter-coup forces began their offensive to retake Vientiane from Savannakhet. These troops from Groupement Tactique (GT) are assembling along Route 13. (Albert Grandolini Collection)

Also advancing along Route 13 was the Groupement Mobile B (GM B), with an armoured squadron attached made up two Chaffee tanks, six Greyhound armoured reconnaissance cars, as well as half-tracks.

In addition to the two motorised task forces advancing along Route 13, the Phoumi forces also committed the Groupe Mobile Spécial 1 (GMS 1), which sailed the Mekong River on landing craft. (Albert Grandolini Collection)

Although little resistance was encountered during their advance along Route 13, the Phoumi forces used their superior firepower by deploying its batteries of 105mm howitzers to suppress the opposition. (Albert Grandolini Collection)

The columns moving along Route 13 were in fact regularly delayed by mines laid by the Neutralist forces. (Albert Grandolini Collection)

Each of the Phoumi columns were accompanied by US Green Berets disguised as civilians of the PEO. (Albert Grandolini Collection)

Meanwhile, there was a disturbing new element to the growing crisis. After Kong Le's coup, the Pathet Lao sent Phoumi Vongvichit to discuss military co-operation with the Neutralist Armed Forces (Forces Armées Neutraliste-FAN). At Abramov's request, Moscow hurriedly ordered the Soviet Air Force's Military Transport Aviation (Voyenno-Transportnoy Aviatsii-VTA) to operate in Laos, and this assigned the 194th Transport Regiment, equipped with Il-14 'Crates', which was allowed to overfly Chinese territory and arrived at Gia Lam Airbase, Hanoi, at the end of November 1960. It was joined by Li-2 Cabs (Russian-made Dakotas) of the 338th Transport Regiment's 2nd Squadron, which remained until 1962 and were then replaced by the regiment's 4th Squadron, as well as elements of the Kirovabad-based 708th Transport Regiment with military markings replaced by civilian registrations. A half-dozen Mil Mi-4 helicopters of a search and rescue flight from Kamchatka were also available.[19] The CIA claimed on 2 January that supplies were apparently flown from the Soviet Union across China into Hanoi in An-12 'Cub' heavy transports, which returned to the Soviet Union in December.[20] The first familiarisation into Vientiane was made on 4 December, and the following day Soviet aircraft began to bring in oil and rice, flying 34 sorties by 14 December, while Beijing supplied POL over land.[21] Soviet Deputy Foreign Minister Georgii Pushkin stated: 'The airlift to Laos has been the highest priority Soviet supply operation since the Second World War'.[22] On 9 December, the Soviets flew in PAVN Major General Chu Huy Man and a 12-man delegation to assess the situation and complete Hanoi's military aid package.

The Pathet Lao's Phoumi Vongvichit now proposed a formal military arrangement between the FAN, the Pathet Lao and North Vietnam. On the morning of 10 December, Phoumi Vongvichit, accompanied by Quinim Pholsena, flew to Hanoi with Deuane, representing Kong Le, in an Air Laos DC-3. The pact was signed within hours and the following morning 'Crate' transports began flying in a PAVN artillery battalion, with four M101 105mm howitzers, six 120mm mortars and 70 PAVN gunners under the command of Major Le Kich. The next day 21 sorties were flown to bring in the remainder of the battalion, with six M101 howitzers and eight 120mm mortars.[23] The Russian build-up continued throughout the remainder of the month, and during the second half of December they flew 180 sorties.

Kong Le Moves North

They arrived in time to bolster Kong Le's troops as Phoumi approached Vientiane from the east. On the afternoon of 13 December, Phoumi's vanguard, wearing green and yellow scarves, linked up with Kouprasith's troops then pushed into Vientiane, as GMS 1 circled north to isolate the city, but heavy artillery fire, some personally directed by Chuy Huy Man, pushed them back.[24] The following afternoon GT arrived with howitzers, by which time Phoumi relieved an 'ill' Kouprasith, placing RM-5 under former RM-3 commander Brigadier Bounphone Marthepharak. With artillery support, Phoumi's men fought their way back into the city to secure the eastern outskirts and the centre.

Kong Le's men were pushed towards the Wattay Airbase, and on the morning of 16 December he reluctantly accepted defeat. Accompanied by PAVN gunners, army and police prisoners, he retreated north up Route 13, establishing a base at the village of Vang Vieng, which had an airfield. Five PAVN advisors flying there by helicopter that day crashed in Thailand but successfully evaded capture and escaped to friendly positions after 56 days. The US Air Attaché, Lieutenant Colonel Butler B. Toland, flying his VC-47 VIP transport over Laos on 16 December personally observed and photographed a 'Crate' parachuting supplies into Vang Vieng, but ground fire damaged his aircraft on 23 December to become the first US aircraft casualty in Laos.

With the fall of Wattay Airbase that afternoon, Vientiane was in Phoumi's hands, but to paraphrase the US Army major's comment about Ben Tre in Tet 1968: 'It became necessary to destroy the capital to save the country'. The city was wrecked, with 7,000 luckless people losing their homes, while 600-1,000 were killed and there were fears of a cholera epidemic. To prevent this, an international airlift was organised to bring in supplies and medical staff. In addition, the CIA's Far Eastern Division chief Desmond 'Dizzy Fits' FitzGerald flew in with Lair, the two delighted with their apparent success after a limited investment.[25]

The crew of the Soviet 194th Transport Regiment pose here in Hanoi-Gia Lam Airbase in early 1961. Like the CIA Air America pilots operating in profit of the Laotian forces, they wore civilian clothes, and their aircraft had all military markings removed. (VPAF)

The most dramatic development was direct Soviet intervention in Laos when Moscow decided, on 11 December 1960, to put in place an air bridge between North Vietnam and Vientiane, bringing in a North Vietnamese artillery battalion and supplies for the Neutralists. The US Air Attaché, Lieutenant Colonel Butler B. Toland, flying his VC-47 VIP transport over Laos on 16 December personally observed and photographed this Soviet Il-14 parachuting supplies into Vang Vieng. (USAF)

On 13 December 1960, the Phoumi forces reached the outskirt of Vientiane. They were engaged in an artillery duel with the North Vietnamese gunners which destroyed a great part of the capital of Laos. (Albert Grandolini Collection)

An M8 armoured car of the GM B of Colonel Ekarath Souvannarot advancing cautiously in the streets of Vientiane. (Albert Grandolini Collection)

Phoumi troops advanced through Vientiane with the support of an 81mm mortar battery. (Albert Grandolini Collection)

A FAL troop passing through a wrecked courtyard and destroyed cars. (Albert Grandolini Collection)

Phoumi troops conquered the whole of Vientiane after a three-day battle, but many parts of the city were badly damaged, like the building of the Laotian Army headquarters. (Albert Grandolini Collection)

The armoured squadron of the RM-5, under Colonel Kouprasith Abhay, who had chosen a neutral attitude at the Chinaimo base, south of Vientiane, was now thrown into the battle to support the Phoumi forces arriving on the outskirts of Vientiane. This group of M24 tanks, M8 armoured cars and half-tracks is advancing towards the centre of the city. (Albert Grandolini Collection)

Kong Le retreated along Route 13 towards the strategic crossroads on the Plain of Jars, making no attempt to hold Phon Hong and abandoning Vang Vieng. To support him the Pathet Lao sent 1,000 troops with more PAVN gunners to dig in around Moung Kassy, while the FAN continued north to take the Route 7 junction at Sala Phou Khoun. Following a feint north to Luang Prabang, Kong Le then pushed eastwards along Route 7 towards the Muong Soui airfield. This was defended by a Hmong guerrilla company, whose resistance was confined to felling trees before they dispersed allowing the FAN to move in, then push onto the Plain of Jars. FAL forces retreated south, the only resistance coming from Hmong ADC forces and theirs was more a fighting retreat to a new sanctuary.

Phoumi, nominally under Boun Oum, promoted himself Major General and tightened his grip on the administration, aided by the new National Directorate for Co-ordination. This controlled both civil and military police forces and purged any real, or suspected, Pathet Lao or Neutralist supporters, yet Phoumi remained so insecure he would sleep at a Thai military base and commute into Vientiane by helicopter. His success was welcomed by Diem in Saigon, who sent corps commander Colonel Nguyen Khanh and divisional commander Lieutenant Colonel Nguyen Van Thieu to propose a joint operation along Route 9 in the Panhandle against the PAVN. But Phoumi's response was lukewarm, and it became clear he was more concerned about the direct threat in northern Laos rather than an indirect one in the south.[26]

In the Plain of Jars, RM-2 commander, and former air commander, Colonel Sourith was driven out of his Xieng Khouang headquarters to Khang Khai on 31 December, despite 300 reinforcements being parachuted in on New Year's Day, as the enemy laid down such a storm of fire they all fled down Route 4. Although Air America attempted to fly in 105mm howitzers, the rapid approach of the FAN saw the defenders evaporating like the morning mist, but the Americans succeeded in evacuating PEO and 'Hotfoot' advisors, as Vang Pao organised a vigorous defence before flying out on the last transport. A mercurial man, he was briefly in despair over the defeat and initially decided to join the Hmong in the south but, having received counter-insurgency training in the Philippines only two years earlier, changed his mind and decided to continue the fight. He began contacting Hmong communities scattered around the Plain of Jars after their leaders, anticipating the plain might be occupied by hostile forces, had dispersed 200 villages with 70,000 people into the surrounding mountains to be supplied by Air America parachute drops.[27]

By New Year's Day 1961, Kong Le controlled the plain's road network and within three days secured the whole region aided by loot from Vientiane, including over 100 vehicles, six 105mm howitzers, seven 120mm mortars, a M24 tank and two M8 armoured vehicles, and he also had a tiny air force consisting of a Dakota and two Beavers.[28] His hold was secured by 'Crates' bringing in 18 pieces of 85mm and 105mm artillery, as well as Chinese military supplies. Despite American pressure, Phoumi was more interested in consolidating his position in Vientiane against his rival Kouprasith than in pursuing Kong Le. On 30 December a plan was drawn up to envelop Vang Vien with some 5,600 men from RM-1, RM-2 and RM-5, but Kong Le's abandonment of the town rendered the plan redundant. Sourith was left with a toehold in RM-2 along Route 4, with two battalions (BI 6, BV 21) at the village of Ta Nieng, some 50 kilometres southeast of Xieng Khouang, near the border with Borikhane province. Three others were on the provincial border at Tha Tom (Muang Thathom), 22 kilometres southeast of Ta Nieng, which Sourith soon lost before moving his headquarters to Paksane in Borikhane.

Hanoi responded to the Phoumi countercoup by authorising 4th Military Region to send PAVN units across the border to support the struggle in the south. Kong Le's occupation of the Plain of Jars led Chu Huy Man to bring a 30-man PAVN liaison team to Khang Khai to co-ordinate operations. On 15 January the 925th Independent Battalion crossed the border and joined a FAN counterattack at Pha Trang, north of Vang Vieng, pushing the FAL forces to Hun Heup, 95 kilometres north of Vientiane. Elements of the battalion then made minor probes north of Paksane, towards Tha Vieng and Tha Thom. Meanwhile, the Pathet Lao strengthened their position in Houa Phan. On 31 December a 2nd PL Battalion company, with 120th PAVN Regiment support, attacked Nong Het, a village just inside Laos on Route 7, driving out the defending company which informed RM-2 headquarters it had faced seven battalions! The PAVN presence certainly increased, with 40 specialists donning Pathet Lao uniforms to join the 6th Pathet Lao Battalion near Vang

Vieng. Group 959 steadily expanded from 160 in late 1960 to 3,085 in mid-1962.[29]

Underpinning this effort was the Russian and North Vietnamese airlift flying to Sam Neua or dropping supplies, all of which was credited by the North Vietnamese with assisting their operations.[30] By delivering up to 50 tonnes a day, they strengthened the Pathet Lao main force units which could now meet those of the FAL on an equal basis.[31]

In late February, Souvanna Phouma flew in a Russian aircraft into Khang Khai from Phnom Penh to meet Souphanouvong and other Pathet Lao leaders. Spurred on by the Pathet Lao, Kong Le created a Neutralist government under Quinim Pholsena, with its capital at Khang Khai. Souvanna found the Soviet embassy, a Chinese 'economic and cultural delegation', a North Vietnamese 'information office' and a field hospital as well as a Czech 'information office' all protected by Russian-supplied, 37mm anti-aircraft guns.[32] Meanwhile, the Pathet Lao and Chuy Huy Man's team began a long, but continuous, process of winning over the Neutralists in a process which would eventually split the movement.

The North Vietnamese Air Force also joined the Soviet air bridge to deliver supplies to the Neutralist and Pathet Lao troops in the Plain of Jars. These three Lisunov Li-2s of the VPAF 919th Transport Regiment are heading towards Laos after taking off from Dien Bien Phu Airbase. Although they had kept their serial numbers, all the national markings had been removed. (VPAF)

A FAL outpost on the fringe of the Plain of jars on Route 13 in February 1961. It was reinforced with a 4.2 inch (107mm) M30 heavy mortar which has just been delivered by an Air America C-46). (Albert Grandolini Collection).

After arriving in the Plain of Jars, part of the BP 2 of Kong Le was equipped with Soviet equipment delivered by Soviet and North Vietnamese aircraft. These paratroopers are armed with Soviet PPSh-41 SMGs. (Albert Grandolini Collection)

BIBLIOGRAPHY

Books and Theses

Ahern, Thomas L. Jr, *Undercover Armies: CIA and Surrogate Warfare in Laos* (Washington, DC: Center for the Study of Intelligence, CIA, 2006)

Ang Cheng Guan, *The Vietnam War from the Other Side: The Vietnamese Communists' Perspective* (London and New York: Routledge Curzon Taylor & Francis, 2002).

Anthony, Victor B. and Richard R. Sexton, *The War in Northern Laos* (Washington DC: Center for Air Force History, United States Air Force, 1993.)

Bowers, Ray L., *Tactical Airlift* (Washington: Office of Air Force History & GPO, 1983).

Blaufarb, Douglas S., *Organizing and Managing Unconventional War in Laos, 1962-1970* (Santa Monica: Advanced Research Projects Agency, RAND Corporation, 1972)

Castle, Timothy N., *At War in the Shadow of Vietnam. US military aid to the Royal Lao Government 1955-1975* (New York: Columbia University Press, 1993)

Cadeau, Ivan; Cochet, François and Porte, Rémy, *La guerre d'Indochine, Dictionnaire* (Paris: Perrin – Ministère des Armées, 2021)

Cattori, Sylvia and Jean, *Asie du Sud-Est, l'Enjeu Thaïlandais* (Paris: Éditions L'Harmattan, 1985)

Celeski, Joseph D., *Special Air Warfare and the Secret War in Laos: Air Commandos 1964–1975* (Maxwell Air Force Base, Alabama: Air University Press Curtis E. LeMay Center for Doctrine Development and Education, 2019)

Clarke, Jeffrey J., *Advice and Support: The Final Years, 1965–1973* (Washington, D.C.: US Army Center of Military History, 1988)

Conboy, Ken, *The Erawan War Vol 1: The CIA Paramilitary Campaign in Laos, 1961-1969* (Warwick: Helion & Co, 2021)

Conboy, Ken, *The Erawan War Vol 2: The CIA Paramilitary Campaign in Laos, 1969-1974* (Warwick: Helion & Co, 2022)

Conboy, Ken, *The Erawan War Vol 3: The Royal Lao Armed Forces, 1961-1974* (Warwick: Helion & Co, 2022)

Conboy, Kenneth, with James Morrison, *Shadow War: The CIA's secret war in Laos* (Boulder, Colorado: Paladin Press, 1995)

Cosmas, Graham A., *MACV: The Joint Command in the Years of Escalation 1962-1967* (Washington DC: Center of Military History, US Army, 2006)

Currey Cecil B., *Victory at Any Cost: The Genius of Vietnam's Gen. Vo Nguyen Giap* (Washington: Brassey's Inc., 1997)

Dassé, Martial, *Les guérillas en Asie du Sud-Est : Les stratégies de la guerre asiatique* (Paris: Éditions L'Harmattan, 1993)

Deuve, Jean, *La guerre secrète au Laos contre les Communistes (1955-1964)* (Paris: Éditions L'Harmattan, 2000)

Deuve, Jean, *Le Royaume du Laos 1949-1965: Histoire évènementielle de l'indépendance à la guerre américaine* (Paris: Éditions L'Harmattan, 2003)

Fall, Bernard B., *Street Without Joy: Insurgency in Indochina 1946-1955* (London: Pall Mall Press, 1965)

Fenton, Damien Marc, *SEATO and the Defence of Southeast Asia 1955-1965* (Canberra, ACT: Thesis for School of Humanities and Social Sciences, University of New South Wales, 2006)

Ferguson, J. Michael, *Air America and the War in Laos, 1959-1974* (Dallas, Texas: Thesis for University of Texas, 2010)

Fleurence, Général Michel *Rotors dans le ciel d'Indochine – Les hommes – Tome 1* (Vincennes: Editeur: SHAA, 2003)

Flintham, Victor, *Air Wars and Aircraft – A detailed record of Air Combat, 1945 to the Present* (London: Arms and Armour Press, 1989)

Freedman, Lawrence, *Kennedy's Wars: Berlin, Cuba, Laos and Vietnam* (New York and Oxford: Oxford University Press, 2000)

Fursenko, Aleksandr and Timothy Naftaly, *Khrushchev's Cold War: The Inside story of an American adversary* (New York, New York: W. W. Norton & Company, 2006)

Futrell, Robert F. and Martin Blumenson, *The United States Air Force in Southeast Asia. The Advisory Years to 1965* (Washington, DC: Office of Air Force History 1980)

Gosha, Christopher and Laplante, Karine, *The failure of Peace in Indochina 1954 – 1962* (Paris: Les Indes Savantes, 2010)

Gras, Général Yves, *Histoire de la Guerre d'Indochine* (Paris: Libraire Plon, 1979)

Gunn, Geoffrey C., *Political Struggles in Laos 1930-1954. Vietnamese Communist power and the Lao struggle for national independence* (Bangkok: Editions Duang Kamal, 1988)

Hofmann, Colonel George R., *Operation Millpond: U.S. Marines in Thailand, 1961* (Quantico, Virginia: History Division, US Marine Corps, 2009)

Hofmann, Colonel George R., *The Path to War: U.S. Marine Corps Operations in Southeast Asia 1961-1965: Marines in the Vietnam War Commemorative Series* (Washington DC: U.S. Government Printing Office, 2014)

Jacobs, Seth, *The Universe Unraveling: American Foreign Policy in Cold War Laos* (Ithaca: Cornell University Press, 2012)

Journaud, Pierre, *De Gaulle et le Vietnam 1945 -1969* (Paris: Editions Tallandier, 2011)

Kelly, Colonel Francis J., *Vietnam Studies: US Army Special Forces 1961-1971* (Washington DC: Department of the Army, 1973)

Kirl, Donald, *Wider War – The struggle for Cambodia, Thailand, and Laos* (New York: Praeger Publishers, 1971)

Langer, P.F. and J.J. Zasloff, *Revolution in Laos: The North Vietnamese and the Pathet Lao* (Santa Monica, The RAND Corporation, 1969)

Lich Su Binh Chung Thiet Giap Quan Doi Nhan Dan Viet Nam 1959 – 1975 – PAVN Armour Corps History 1959 – 1975 (Ha Noi: Nha Xuat Ban Quan Doi Nhan Dan, 1982).

Lich Su Cong Binh Viet Nam 1945 – 1975 – PAVN Engineer Corps History 1945-1975 (Ha Noi, Nha Xuat Ban Quan Doi Nhan Dan, 1991).

Lich Su Quan Chung Phao Binh 1945 – 1975 – *PAVN Artillery Corps History 1945 – 1975* (Ha Noi: Nha Xuat Ban Quan Doi Nhan 1991).

Lich Su Quan Chung Phong Khong – PAVN Air Defence Command History, 2 vols (Hanoi: Nha Xuat Ban Quan Doi Nhan 1991 and 1993).

Lich Su Quan He Dac Biet Viet Nam – Lao; 1930 – 2007 – Special Relationship between Vietnam and Laos History 1930 – 2007 (Ha Noi: Nha Xuat Ban Chinh Tri Quoc Gia, 2007).

Lich Su Bo Doi Truong Son Duong Ho Chi Minh –Troops of the Ho Chi Minh Trails History (Ha Noi: Nha Xuat Ban Quan Doi Nhan Dan, 1994).

Lien-Hang T. Nguyen, *Hanoi's War: An International History of the War for Peace in Vietnam* (Chapel Hill: University of North Carolina Press, 2012).

McDonnell, Major Wayne W., *The NVA in Laos 1951-73* (Fort Leavenworth, Kansas: US Army Command and General Staff College Thesis, 1977)

The Military History Institute of Vietnam, Pribbenow, Merle L. (Translator), *Victory in Vietnam: The official history of the People's Army of Vietnam 1954-1975* (Lawrence, Kansas: University of Kansas Press, 2002)

Murfett, Malcolm H., (Editor) *Cold War Southeast Asia* (Tarrytown, NY; Marshall Cavendish Editions, Singapore; and Marshall Cavendish Corp., 2012)

O'Ballance, Edgar, *The Indo-China War 1945-1954: A study in Guerrilla Warfare* (London; Faber & Faber, 1964)

Pham Phong Dinh, *Chien Su Quan Luc Viet Nam Cong Hoa – One chapter for each division, and each other major component of the RVNAF, in the 1970s* (Winnipeg: Tu Sach Vinh Danh, 2001)

Pike, Douglas, *PAVN: People's Army of Vietnam* (London: Brassey's Defence Publishers, 1986)

Prados, John, *The Blood Road: The Ho Chi Minh Trail and the Vietnam War* (New York, New York: John Wiley & Sons, Inc, 1999)

Qiang Zhai, *China and the Vietnam Wars, 1950-1975* (Chapel Hill, NC: The University of North Carolina Press, 2000)

Randolph, R. Sean, *The United States and Thailand Alliance Dynamics, 1950-1985: Research Papers and Policy Studies 12* (Berkeley, California: Institute of East Asian Studies, University of California, 1986)

Sananikone, Major General Oudane, *The Royal Lao Army and US Army Advice and Support* (Washington, DC: The US Army Center of Military History, 1984)

Schlight, John, *A War Too Long: The USAF in Southeast Asia 1961-1975* (Washington DC: US Air Force History and Museums Program, US Government Printing Office, 1996)

Schulimson, Jack, *The Joint Chiefs of Staff and the War in Vietnam: Part 1 1960-1968* (Washington DC: Office of Joint History, Office of the Chairman of the Joint Chiefs of Staff, 2011)

Stanton, Shelby L., *Vietnam Order of Battle* (Washington, DC: US News Books, 1981)

Stanton, Shelby L., *Green Berets at War. US Special Forces in Southeast Asia 1956-1975* (Novato, California: Presidio Press, 1985)

Stuart-Fox, Martin, *A History of Laos* (Cambridge: Cambridge University Press, 1997)

Taylor, General Maxwell, *Swords and Ploughshares: A Memoir* (New York, New York: W.W. Norton & Company, 1972)

Thayer, Carlyle A., *War By Other Means: National liberation and revolution in Viet-Nam 1954-60* (Sydney; Allen & Unwin Australia, 1989)

Trest, Warren A. and TSgt Charles E. Garland, *USAF Operations from Thailand-1966: Counterinsurgency in Thailand* (HQ PACAF, Directorate, Tactical Evaluation, CHECO (Contemporary Historical Examination of Current Operations) Division, November 1967)

Tu Dien Bach Khoa Quan Su Viet Nam – Vietnamese Military Dictionary (Ha Noi: Bo Quoc Phong Nha Xuat Ban Quan Doi Nhan Dan, 1996).

Warner, Roger, *Back Fire: The CIA's Secret War in Laos and its Link to the War in Vietnam* (New York, New York: Simon & Schuster, 1995)

Zhai, Qiang, *China & the Vietnam Wars 1950-1975* (Chapen Hill, North Carolina: The University of North Carolina Press, 2000

Articles

Bodin, Michel, *L'utilisations des autochtones dans le corps expéditionnaire français en Extrême-Orient*, Revue Française d'Histoire d'Outre-Mer, Tome LXXXI (Nr 303) June 1994, pp.137-159

Césari, Laurent, *Une cause méconnue de la guerre du Vietnam, la neutralisation du Laos*, Bulletin de l'Institut d'Histoire du Temps Présent, no.34 (June 1996), pp.157-168

Czyzak, John J. and Carl F. Salans, *The International Conference on the Settlement of the Laotian Question and the Geneva Agreements of 1962*, The American Journal of International Law. Volume 57/2 (April 1963) pp.300–317

James K. Galbraith, *Exit Strategy: In 1963, JFK ordered a complete withdrawal from Vietnam*, Boston Review, Volume 28, No.5 (October/November 2003)

Grandolini, Albert, *Criquet sur Vientiane*, Le fana de l'Aviation 256 (March 1991), pp.38-41

Grandolini, Albert, *Les blindés communistes dans la guerre du Vietnam*, Tank Zone Magazine Number 12 (August-Septembre 2010), pp.62-80

Goscha, Christopher E., *Vietnam and the World Outside: The case of Vietnamese Communist advisors in Laos (1948-1962)*, South East Asia Research, Volume 12 (2004), Issue 2, pp.141-185

Goscha, Christopher E., *Une Guerre pour l'Indochine? Le Laos et le Cambodge dans le conflit franco-vietnamien (1948-1954)*, Guerres mondiales et conflits contemporains 211 (2003/3), pp.29-58

Leary, William M., *CIA Air Operations in Laos, 1955-1974*, Studies in Intelligence, Vol 43/3 (Winter 1999-2000), pp.51-67

Michaels, Jeffrey H., *Managing Global Counterinsurgency: The Special Group (CI) 1962–1966*, Journal of Strategic Studies, Vol 35, Issue 1, pp.33-61

Le Page, Jean-Marc, *La base de Séno, la France et l'Asie du Sud-Est (1953-1963)*, Guerres mondiales et conflits contemporains Volume 255, 3/2014 (September), pp.123-141

Osornprasop, Sutayut, *Thailand and the Secret War in Laos*, Lao, Southeast Asia and the Cold War, pp.186-214

Documents

CIA Files

C02066875: Central Intelligence Bulletin 2 January 1961

C02000177: Central Intelligence Bulletin 21 January 1961

C02000178: Central Intelligence Bulletin 23 January 1961

C02049782: Central Intelligence Bulletin 8 May 1961

CO3172686: Central Intelligence Bulletin 25 May 1961

NLK-02-35C: Summary of actions authorised by President Kennedy on 9 March 1961

OCI 1541/63: Resupply efforts for Kong Le and Meo Forces in Plaine des Jarres Area, 2 May 1963

RDP64B00346R000300220017-1: Laos, January 1963

RDP65B00383R000400040003-3; CIA Support to Meo Tribesmen in Laos, 8 April 1963

RPD79-00927A003200010001-6: Current Weekly Intelligence Summary, 27 April 1961

RDP79S00427A000100050034-7: The Situation in Laos, 20 April 1961

RDP80B01676R000400080012-9: 'Would the Loss of South Vietnam and Laos Precipitate a "Domino Effect" in the Far East?', 9 June 1964

RDP80R01443R000200220001-6: Military situation throughout Indochina, 6 April 1954

Websites

25th Infantry Division Association web site (https) (www) 25thida.org/units/infantry

Bodin, Michel, *Les laotiens dans la guerre d'Indochine, 1945-1954*, Revue des Guerres Mondiales et Conflits Contemporains 230 (2/2008) pp. 5-21, (https) (www) cairn.info/revue-guerres-mondiales-et-conflits-contemporains-2008-2-page 5.htm

Leeker, Dr Joe E., *Air America aircraft*, University of Texas at Dallas, 2003-2015, (https) somwritinglab.utdallas.edu/library/specialcollections/hac/cataam/Leeker/aircraft

Roberts, Priscilla, *The British Royal Air Force: Operations over Laos against the Ho Chi Minh Trail, 1962*, Cold War International History Project, History and Public Policy program, (https) (www) wilsoncenter.org/publication/ the-british-royal-air-force-operations-over-laos-against-the-ho-chi-minh-trail-1962/

US Marine Corps History Division, (https) (www) usmcu.edu/Research/Marine-Corps-History-Division/People/Whos-Who-in-Marine-Corps-History/Paige-Russell/Lieutenant-General-Carson-Abel-Roberts.

US Navy History and Heritage Command, *By Sea, Air, and Land. Chapter 2: The Era of Growing Conflict, 1959-1965*, (https) (www) history.navy.mil/library/online-reading-room/

ENDNOTES

Prologue

1 The Chinese also accepted the domino theory Zhai, *China & the Vietnam Wars* p.94. Hereafter Zhai.
2 Goscha, *Vietnam and the World Outside* p.153. Hereafter Goscha.

Chapter 1

1 For Laotian history see Conboy & Morrison, *Shadow War* pp.viii, ix, 1-6, 8-10. Hereafter Conboy/Morrison. Stuart-Fox, *A History of Laos* pp.6-70, 74-75. Hereafter Stuart-Fox.
2 Muang Phon-hong became the capital in 1989.
3 Dassé, *Les Guerrillas en Asie du Sud-Est*, p.64. Hereafter Dassé.
4 For the organisation of the Lao Issara forces see *Lich Su Quan He Dac Biet Vietnam-Lao* pp.22-24. Hereafter Lich Su VL. See also Stuart-Fox pp.63-64.
5 Deuve. *Le Royaume du Laos*, pp.28-30. Hereafter Deuve, Royaume.
6 Dassé. p.65.
7 For Pathet Lao forces see Conboy/Morrison pp.3-4.
8 For political activity Gunn, *Political Struggles in Laos* pp.133-274. Hereafter Gunn.
9 Lich Su VL pp.25-26.
10 Lich Su VL pp.28-29.
11 Lich Su VL pp.30-32. PAVN was officially created on 22 December 1944 even that thereafter it changed its name several times to suit local political conditions, but it was always referred internally as the PAVN. The PAVN name was finally reinstated officially on 12 December 1964. The term Viet Minh was commonly used for both the movement and its forces into the 1960s.

Chapter 2

1 Lich Su VL pp.33-34.
2 Stuart-Fox p.79.
3 Stuart-Fox pp.79-80.
4 Lich Su VL p.35
5 Stuart-Fox p.77.
6 Stuart-Fox p.81.
7 Lich Su VL p.37.
8 For the war see Fall, *Street Without Joy*; Gras, *Histoire de la Guerre d'Indochine*; O'Ballance, *The Indo-China War* and also Zhai.
9 Bodin article *l'Utulisations des Autochtones dans le Corps Expéditionnaire Français en Extrême-Orient* p.145.
10 For the Laotian Army see Conboy/Morrison pp.4, 6-8; Oudane Sananikone, *The Royal Lao Army and US Army Advice and Support* pp.14-30 Hereafter Sananikone.
11 For the Laotian forces during the First Indochina War see Bodin web site *Les laotiens dans la guerre d'Indochine*; For the Hmong in the French Indochina war see McDonnell, *The NVA in Laos 1951-73* p.1, 3-4. Hereafter McDonnell.
12 For operations in Laos 1953-1954 see Conboy/Morrison pp.4-6, 8-10; Fall pp.114-116, 119-121, 185; Gras pp.496-499, 521-528; O'Ballance, pp.186-189, 191-192, 209-211; Lich Su VL p.42.
13 Lich Su VL pp.38-39.
14 Lich Su VL p.40.
15 For Viet Minh operations in Laos related to the Dien Bien Phu Battle, see Lich Su VL pp.44-46.
16 CIA-RDP80R01443R000200220001-6.
17 CIA-RDP80B01676R000400080012-9.
18 Fleurence, *Rotors dans le ciel d'Indochine*, pp.471-501.
19 Deuve, *La guerre secrète au Laos contre les Communistes* p.16. Hereafter Deuve, Secrete.
20 For the base see article Le Page, *La base de Séno* f/n 2. Hereafter Le Page. See f/n.2 for the name.
21 Cattori, *Asie du Sud-Est, l'Enjeu Thailandais*, p.66.

Chapter 3

1 Goscha pp.149-150.
2 Goscha pp.165-166.
3 Lich Su VL p.47. See also Goscha pp.170-174.
4 Lich Su VL pp.48-49.
5 For the Moung Peun battle see Conboy/Morrison pp.16-17, 27 f/n 20.
6 Conboy/Morrison p. 16-17. Siyanon became Director General of the Royal Thai Police in July 1957 which he dual-hatted with his position as Interior Minister from March 1957. When dictator Phibun was overthrown in September 1957, Phao fled to Switzerland where he died in 1960.
7 Conboy/Morrison p.18.
8 For Laotian forces after Geneva see Conboy/Morrison pp.14-16, p.27 f/n 10, 14, 16, 24, p. 28 f/n 53; Conboy, *Erawan 3* pp.2-5, 8; Sananikone pp.32-44, 80.
9 Conboy/Morrison pp.17, 55 f/n 28; Sananikone p.44. *Rapport parlementaire Juin 1966, aide militaire française au Laos.*
10 Until 1962 the M101 was known as the M2, but the post 1962 designation will be retained in this work.
11 For the AVRL and MRL see Conboy, *The Erawan War* Vol 3 pp.50-54, 64-67. Hereafter Conboy, *Erawan 3*.
12 Conboy/Morrison p.14
13 Conboy/Morrison p.14; Sananikone pp.34-4.
14 Goscha pp.163-164, 168-170; McDonnell pp.5-6; Lich Su VL p.47.
15 For Laos between 1954 and 1958 see Castle, *At War in the Shadow of Vietnam* pp.46-47, Hereafter Castle; Conboy/Morrison pp.13-14, 18-19, 21, 28 f/n 35, 28 f/n 36; Stuart-Fox, pp.84-90, 94-108.
16 Osornprasop, *Thailand and the Secret War in Laos* p.193. Hereafter Osornprasop; Stuart-Fox p.63-64.
17 Stuart-Fox pp.93-94.
18 Lich Su VL p.49.
19 Osornprasop p.192.

20 Goscha pp.166-167.
21 Conboy/Morrison p.18, p.27 n 4, 31.
22 Conboy/Morison p.17; Conboy, *The Erawan Wars* Vol 1 p.3. Hereafter Conboy, *Erawan 1*.
23 Castle pp.43-44; Ferguson, *Air America and the War in Laos*, p.3. Hereafter Ferguson; Stuart-Fox pp.90-93. For the background to American policy in Laos in late 1950s see Jacobs, *The Universe Unraveling* pp.50-81, 136-144. Hereafter Jacobs.
24 Césari article, *Une cause méconnue de la guerre du Vietnam, la neutralisation du Laos*, p.158. Hereafter Césari.
25 Deuve, Royaume p.82.
26 Conboy/Morrison pp.17-18.
27 Goscha pp.164, 170.
28 Goscha p.166.
29 Goscha p.168.
30 Goscha p.163.
31 Stuart-Fox p.91.
32 For the PAVN see Conboy/Morrison p.27 f/n 17; McDonnell pp.6-7.
33 Goscha pp.174-175; McDonnell pp.8-9, 18-19.
34 Castle pp.20, 22-24; Stuart-Fox p.90.

Chapter 4

1 For political events in 1959 see Castle pp.46-47; Conboy/Morrison pp.25-26; Stuart-Fox pp.105-108.
2 Stuart-Fox p.107.
3 Osornprasop p.193.
4 Conboy, *Erawan 3* pp.6-7; Military History Institute of Vietnam, *Victory in Vietnam* p.73. Hereafter Victory.
5 Conboy/Morrison p.23.
6 Stuart-Fox p.109.
7 For the US in Laos see Castle pp.44-45; Conboy/Morrison pp.13, 17-18; Conboy, *Erawan 3* p.5; Stuart-Fox pp.90, 94-98, 103-105.
8 Hoffman, *The Path to War* pp.16-17. Hereafter Hoffman.
9 For the coup and the subsequent crisis see Castle pp.49-51; Conboy/Morrison pp.25-26, 31; Stuart-Fox pp.109-112.
10 Air America was created in February 1959 and nominally absorbed CAT assets on 10 July but CAT continued in semi-autonomy and aircraft in its livery were operating over Laos until early 1962.
11 Lich Su VL p.50.
12 For the Pathet Lao 'mutiny' and its aftermath see Conboy/Morrison pp.13-14, 18, 21; Conboy, *Erawan 3* pp.7-8; Jacobs pp.144-45; Stuart-Fox pp.99-103, 107-108.
13 Lich Su VL p.51.
14 Goscha p.175-179; McDonnell p.7-8.
15 McDonnell pp. 13-14, 19-20.
16 For these events see Conboy/Morrison pp.21-22; Conboy, *Erawan 3* pp.7-8; Langer & Zasloff, *Revolution in Laos* pp 90-99. Hereafter Langer/Zasloff; Stuart-Fox pp.108-109; Lich Su VL p.52.
17 For Faidang see Stuart-Fox pp.30, 71-73, 94.
18 Stuart-Fox p.111.
19 Deuve, Secret pp121-125.
20 See Conboy/Morrison p. 22; Stuart-Fox p.109.
21 For AD see Conboy/Morrison p.23, p.29 n.65; Conboy, *Erawan 3* p.9.
22 Warner p.23.
23 For the US and foreign expansion see Castle pp.47-49, 84; Conboy/Morrison pp.20-21, 23-24, 28 f/n 49; Jacobs pp.146-147.
24 Kelly, *U.S. Army Special Forces* p.4. Hereafter Kelly; Stanton, *Green Berets at War* pp.5, 12, 16-32. Hereafter Stanton, Berets. See also Clarke, *Advice and Support* p.69. Hereafter Clarke. He notes: 'The individual Special Forces soldier also was viewed as a ground-level exporter of the American way of life and as a sort of folk hero in the tradition of the American frontiersman'.
25 In June 2023 Fort Bragg was renamed Fort Liberty by the Biden Administration but the name was restored by President Trump in February 2025.
26 For 'Hotfoot' see Conboy, *Erawan 3* pp.6, 8.
27 US Navy History and Heritage Command web site, The Era of Growing Conflict.
28 Conboy, *Erawan 3* pp.5-6
29 For JTF 116 and Roberts visit see Conboy/Morrison p.22. For Carson see biography on Marine Corps University web site which notes Carson returned to the United States in December to command the 3d Marine Aircraft Wing. It makes no mention of JTF 116.

Chapter 5

1 For the background see Pike, *PAVN: People's Army of Vietnam*, pp.42-48. Hereafter Pike, PAVN; Prados, *The Blood Road* pp.8-14. Hereafter Prados; Thayer, *War By Other Means*. Hereafter Thayer; Victory pp.4, 10-17, 27, 42-52, 79.
2 Victory p.42.
3 Thayer pp.183-189.
4 Prados p.9.
5 Victory p.41.
6 Prados pp.9-10.
7 Victory p.79.
8 Victory p.52.
9 Conboy/Morrison p.115, 122 n.1.
10 Césari, p.159; Osornprasop p.194.
11 For the Kong Le coup and its aftermath see Castle pp.51-53; Conboy/Morrison pp.31-37, 57-59, p.45 n.11, 23 & 24; Conboy, *Erawan 3* p.10; Goscha pp.179-180; Jacobs pp.155-158; Stuart-Fox pp.112-114, 220 f/n 42; Warner p.24.
12 Conboy/Morrison p.34; Castle p.55.
13 For US reactions see Ahern, *Undercover armies* pp.13-14. Hereafter Ahern; Conboy/Morison p.34; Conboy, *Erawan 1* pp.2-4; Castle pp.49-50, 53-55; Anthony and Sexton, *The war in northern Laos* p.31. Hereafter Anthony/Sexton; Stuart-Fox pp.114-115; Warner p.26.
14 For China see Zhai pp.95-98.
15 Fursenko & Naftaly, *Khrushchev's Cold War*, pp.333.
16 For the PARU see Osornprasop pp.195-197.
17 For Lair see Conboy/Morrison pp.57-59; Warner pp.29-33.
18 For the counter-coup see Castle pp.56-60; Conboy/Morrison pp.34, 36-45, 67, p.46 n.28-51; Conboy, *Erawan 3* p.11; Freedman, *Kennedy's Wars* pp.294-295. Hereafter Freedman; Jacobs pp.129-136, 159-170; Stanton, Berets pp.20-21, 25; Stuart-Fox pp.115-117; Warner pp.29-33.
19 A CIA bulletin of 21 January 1961 noted the Soviet Union had just delivered 18 Li-2 to Haiphong bringing its strength in North Vietnam to 10 Il-14, 18 Li-2 and five Mi-4 helicopters. CIA C02000177 January 21.
20 CIA C02066875.
21 Article, *Quan su Viet Nam, cua chuyen gia khong Lien Xo trong trien tranh chong my*, pp.1-4. Zhai p.96.
22 Osornprasop p.194.
23 Lich Su VL p.53. Castle pp.56-60; Deuve, Royaume p.192; Goscha pp.179-180. Victory p. 87 specifically says an artillery battalion. Stuart-Fox p.116 says only three howitzers and three mortars were delivered.
24 Goscha p.179.
25 Warner pp.32-33.
26 Conboy/Morrison p.115; Stuart-Fox p.118.
27 For the capture of the Plain of Jars Castle p.96; Conboy/Morrison pp.43-44, 47-48,60-61; Conboy, *Erawan 3* pp.11-14; Stuart-Fox p.117.
28 Deuve, Le Royaume pp.201-204.
29 For PAVN intervention see Conboy/Morrison p.50; Goscha pp.179-182; McDonnell pp. 16-17; Stuart-Fox p.118; CIA C02066875.
30 Goscha p.182.
31 For CIA reports on the airlift see CIA bulletins C02066875; C02000177 of 2, 21 and 23 January 1961.
32 Castle p.75.

ABOUT THE AUTHOR

Albert Grandolini
Military historian and aviation journalist, Albert Grandolini was born in Vietnam and gained an MA in history from Paris I Sorbonne University. His primary research focus on contemporary conflicts in general and particularly on the military history of Asia and Africa. Having spent his childhood in South Vietnam, the Vietnam War as well as the revolutionary conflicts in Asia have always been one of his main fields of research. He has authored numerous books for Helion's Asia@war and Africa@war Series. He has also written numerous articles for various British, French, and German magazines.

Ted Hooton
E.R. (Ted) Hooton is a retired defence journalist who worked for 30 years for Monch and Janes before establishing the Spyglass newsletters. Since retirement he has focused upon military history, being a member of the British Commission for Military History, and has written some two dozen books, many of them highly regarded. These have covered the Chinese Civil War, the Luftwaffe, the Spanish Civil War (two books), the Balkan Wars as well as air operations over the Western Front (1916-1918) and the Eastern Front (1941-1945).